24/DIA

"Morality — is there really a right and a wrong? 'Who cares? People can decide for themselves as long as it doesn't hurt anybody. It's a free country.' Been there! Heard that! Come, sit at the feet of a master storyteller who unpacks how God created life to work. You will be the one set free."

— JOEL HOUSHOLDER, TH.M., director of Search Ministries, Dallas; national speaker on marriage and family with Family Life; 20-year veteran with Young Life; father of three, husband of one

STICKING UP FOR WHAT IS RIGHT

ANSWERS TO THE MORAL DILEMMAS TEENAGERS FACE

Gwendolyn Mitchell Diaz

NAVPRESS

BRINGING TRUTH TO LIFE
P.O. Box 35001, Colorado Springs, Colorado 80935

OUR GUARANTEE TO YOU

The Navigators is an international Christian organization. Our mission is to reach, disciple, and equip people to know Christ and to make Him known through successive generations. We envision multitudes of diverse people in the United States and every other nation who have a passionate love for Christ, live a lifestyle of sharing Christ's love, and multiply spiritual laborers among those without Christ.

NavPress is the publishing ministry of The Navigators. NavPress publications help believers learn biblical truth and apply what they learn to their lives and ministries. Our mission is to stimulate spiritual formation among our readers.

© 2002 by Gwendolyn Diaz

All rights reserved. No part of this publication may be reproduced in any form without written permission from NavPress, P.O. Box 35001, Colorado Springs, CO 80935. www.navpress.com

ISBN 1-57683-312-7

Cover design by Ray Moore
Cover photo by Getty Images Creative / Image Bank 10131690
Creative Team: Paul Santhouse, Greg Clouse, Darla Hightower, Glynese Northam

Some of the anecdotal illustrations in this book are true to life and are included with the permission of the persons involved. All other illustrations are composites of real situations, and any resemblance to people living or dead is coincidental.

Unless otherwise identified, all Scripture quotations in this publication are taken from the HOLY BIBLE: NEW INTERNATIONAL VERSION® (niv®). Copyright © 1973, 1978, 1984 by International Bible Society. Used by permission of Zondervan Publishing House. All rights reserved.

Diaz, Gwendolyn Mitchell.
   Sticking up for what is right : answers to the moral dilemmas
teenagers face / by Gwendolyn Mitchell Diaz.
      p. cm.
Includes bibliographical references.
   ISBN 1-57683-312-7
1. Christian ethics. 2. Teenagers--Religious life. I. Title.
BJ1249 .D48 2002
241--dc21
                                    2002008209

Printed in the United States of America

1 2 3 4 5 6 7 8 9 10 / 05 04 03 02

FOR A FREE CATALOG OF
NAVPRESS BOOKS & BIBLE STUDIES,
CALL 1-800-366-7788 (USA)
OR 1-416-499-4615 (CANADA)

DEAR PARENT,

This book is the second in a series based on discussions with my four sons: Zachary, Matthew, Benjamin, and Jonathan. Like the first, it is written for them based on the experiences that we shared together, but they have said that I may share it with you. Read it yourself to better grasp the moral dilemmas that are challenging your teens and preteens; borrow the ideas and fill in your own stories to share at appropriate moments; or loan it to your kids to read by themselves. There is no better place to honestly confront the moral dilemmas facing our culture and society than in the home.

GWENDOLYN MITCHELL DIAZ

CONTENTS

INTRODUCTION:
Why Are You Trying to Tell Me
How to Live My Life? — 9

DILEMMA #1:
Aren't Right and Wrong Really
Up to the Individual? — 15

DILEMMA #2:
Why Should I Live a Moral Life in
Such an Immoral Society? — 27

DILEMMA #3:
How Can I Live a Moral Life in
Such an Immoral Society? — 41

DILEMMA #4:
Exactly How Honest Am I Supposed to Be? — 53

DILEMMA #5:
What About Sex — How Far Is Too Far? — 67

DILEMMA #6:
Isn't Homosexuality a Valid Lifestyle
Alternative? — 83

DILEMMA #7:
What's the Big Deal About Abortion? Isn't
It a Woman's Right to Decide What to
Do with Her Own Body? — 101

DILEMMA #8:
    Can't I Just See for Myself What's Wrong with
    Drugs and Alcohol? I Won't Become Addicted!   → 115

DILEMMA #9:
    Why Are You So Concerned About Our
    Music, Modems, and the Media?
    It's Only Entertainment!   → 129

DILEMMA #10:
    What If I've Already Blown It?   → 143

DISCUSSION QUESTIONS   151

NOTES   157

ABOUT THE AUTHOR   159

INTRODUCTION

WHY ARE YOU TRYING TO TELL
Me How to Live My Life

JUST AFTER DAD AND I WERE MARRIED, A BEAUTIFUL, BLACK PUPPY WITH big, white paws bounded into our hearts and lives. He was part Labrador retriever and part who-knows-what. We named him Benji. That dog was completely full of energy and mischief! From the moment he greeted us by spreading our clean laundry all over our living room floor until the day we had to say goodbye three years later, he wreaked havoc in our lives!

We lived in an old part of Dallas, right across the street from the school Dad attended. Because there were many tall trees and more than a few thoughtless students in the vicinity, the gutters and the sewer drains often became clogged with leaves and papers. Following a storm, huge puddles flooded the sidewalks and turned the parking lots into shallow ponds.

I have to admit that sometimes I noticed the dirt and debris collecting on the grates when the weather was dry, but I never considered cleaning them off. After all, it wasn't my job to remove trash. People were paid to do that. Why should I get my hands dirty?

One day the school held a very special ladies' luncheon. Everyone who attended was dressed in her Sunday best. I remember wearing a long black-and-white checkered skirt with a peasant blouse. (It was considered chic at the time. Really!) Anyway, during the luncheon it rained, and by the time everyone was ready to leave, there were puddles everywhere.

As I was crossing the street to go home, I heard loud shrieks coming from the parking lot behind me. I turned around just in time to see an extremely filthy ball of dripping wet, black fur running around and leaping. Somebody's dog was enthusiastically greeting each lady as she headed to her car. Mud ricocheted everywhere as the mangy mutt shook itself in sheer delight! Women were lifting their skirts and leaping over puddles to escape the flying filth.

I covered my face in embarrassment and shame when I realized that it was Benji prancing through the mud puddles and flinging sludge all over those beautiful dresses. I didn't know what to do. I stood still — completely paralyzed for a few minutes. Then I sneaked into the house and pretended I was in no way connected with the incident.

Looking back, I realize I might have done many things to prevent that muddy melee — but I chose not to get involved.

First of all, I should have been more community-minded. I should have taken an active role in removing the debris that blocked the grates and kept the water from draining. But that would have taken a lot of time and effort, and it wasn't an appealing way for me to expend my energy after a long day at work.

Before I left for the luncheon, I should have made sure that the gate to our yard was securely fastened so that Benji couldn't get out. But I was in too big a hurry, and I forgot to check it.

When I realized that it was starting to rain, I should have rushed home and put my dog on the porch. That way he never would have been enticed to play in the water and mud.

When I saw Benji prancing in the parking lot, I should have swallowed my pride and called him away from the ladies. But I was too embarrassed to acknowledge my role in the fiasco — and I didn't want to risk ruining my own skirt.

INTRODUCTION

I know I should have owned up to those women that it was my dog that created the mess, and I should have apologized. But I couldn't bring myself to do it. To this day, only a few of my friends know the truth about the incident!

I told you that story because recently I realized that *you* are in the same situation as Benji and those women on that fall day in Dallas. The worst part of this realization is that I am at fault in this situation too. So I want to start this book by apologizing to you, as I should have done to those ladies twenty-some years ago.

I apologize for the terrible, dirty mess that my generation has created and then caused you to grow up in. We recognize how bad it is—we walk past it every day. But I guess we keep waiting for someone else to clean it up. We certainly don't want to get our own hands dirty in the process!

I apologize that we have left the gates of our homes wide open, giving you the freedom to wander around in a world filled with muck. You are free to face an Internet bursting with pornography; read magazines and watch television shows that vie for your attention by promoting sex and violence; and play video games that degrade human life in the name of fun. It makes me shudder when I realize that you cannot do school research, relax in our family room, or run to the grocery store without being enticed to play in puddles filled with such trash and debris.

I apologize that we have been so distant and distracted as adults that your generation has had to grow up apart from our influence and interference. For the first time in American history, kids your age are looking to their peers for guidance rather than to the adults in their world. It's our fault that you have been left alone to wallow in the waste.

Because we feel guilty for spending so little time and effort supervising your growth, we try to compensate by throwing money at you. Big corporations have picked up on this, and every year you are now targeted as an "industry" that is worth over $150 billion to them. And nothing is out of bounds in their quest to snatch your money. They study the ideals you have adopted (without our input) and the rules you have created (apart from our influence), then try to sell you on a souped-up, sex-filled version of the images you are straining to attain.

I apologize that we have deluded your generation into believing that truth is not absolute — that appropriate behavior is dependent on each situation you encounter. Your morality is no longer based on objective standards. You have decided to base it on individual needs and the desire for fulfillment. Therefore, it has become acceptable to lie, cheat, and steal in your world. Personal gratification and advancement are the only justifications needed for most activities.

I apologize that after doing nothing to guide or help you, we are now embarrassed by your behavior, and that after all our failures as parents, we have the blatant audacity to question why *you* are getting mud stains on our clothing and carpets! We, the adults who created your dilemma, have the nerve to sit around piously shocked at the levels of moral illiteracy in your generation.

It's time for us to clean things up. That's why I'm writing this book. But I need your help. Together we need to clean off the debris that clogs the gutters and the grates in our lives. Any time we see dirt we need to make an effort to remove it. We need to start closing the gates that have been left wide open — the gates that allow you to wander into places of dirt and danger. Through this book I want to show you the parameters that will allow your life to remain clean and beautiful in God's eyes so that you can enjoy the peace and joy that He promises to those who trust Him and His Word. If you are already dirty and covered with filth, I want to hand you a towel that will clean you off — the towel of God's love and forgiveness and restoration.

Did you know that no society has survived past the third generation once moral decay has set in? That's a pretty scary thought, isn't it? We *have to* clean things up if we are going to provide a safe place for *your* children to live and play.

DILEMMA #1

AREN'T RIGHT AND WRONG
Really Up to the Individual?

OVER THE SOUNDS OF THE DISHWASHER AND THE GARBAGE DISPOSAL, I could hear the argument escalating in the family room.

"My tower is the biggest."

"Uh-uh, mine's lots bigger than yours!"

"It just looks like it is, 'cause you built yours on the fireplace ledge and mine's down on the floor. But mine's way taller! See, it comes up past my legs."

"Yeah, but your legs are short!"

"I'll knock yours down, then we'll see whose is tallest!"

"Yeah, and then I'll . . ."

"Guys, guys, guys," I interrupted as I rushed into the family room to halt any impending pounding. "What's the problem in here?"

"Ben thinks his tower is taller than mine," Jonathan informed me with a pout. "But it's not! He just started building it on the fireplace ledge so it looks taller, but that doesn't count!"

Do you guys remember this argument? Before it could develop any further, I intervened. "I know how we can tell for sure whose tower is tallest. Ben, why don't you run and get the measuring stick from the pantry? Then we can measure them both."

Ben darted off and returned with the yardstick. He immediately proceeded to measure the skyscraper he had constructed on the hearth. It was thirty-two inches tall. "Ha!" he stated proudly as he handed the ruler to his brother. "Bet yours is less than thirty inches!"

Jonathan measured his tower. It was close. Very close. But careful observation revealed that Jonathan's tower was slightly over thirty-three inches — and therefore slightly taller than Ben's. There was no way to dispute the findings. The yardstick couldn't lie. No matter how many times we measured, it always came out the same. It didn't matter that Ben's position on the raised hearth gave him a different perspective or that he had used more blocks (which were all of different sizes). The truth was that Jonathan's tower was taller than Ben's — until Ben removed the top block from Jonathan's building and placed it on his own!

The yardstick provided an indisputable standard of measurement. It helped us establish order and maintain a relative sense of tranquility in our home that day.

WE HAVE AN INTERNAL DESIRE TO ESTABLISH STANDARDS

Our lives revolve around standards. Something inside us seems driven to establish them. Think about it. We have standards that measure dimensions and distances, standards that assess the quality of our air and water, standards that calculate appropriate chemical balances and determine inappropriate noise levels, standards that test our knowledge and levels of skill, standards that appraise growth and development, standards that judge our actions and time our reactions. I could go on and on. We have established standards to measure and justify and help us enjoy just about every aspect of life.

I don't think we could function without the standards we have established and adopted as a culture and a society. Our world would be in chaos! Imagine how hard it would be to "pay at the pump" if there was no way to measure gasoline. And how could we buy a pair of tennis shoes if they didn't come in sizes? Or how would you know when the bell was supposed to ring at school if you didn't have a watch?

But we seldom stop to realize that all of the standards we establish point to the fact that a Higher Source of standards exists somewhere outside our capabilities. Let me give you some examples that will make that statement a little clearer.

We have chosen to define time by dividing it into increments of seasons, hours, minutes, and even seconds. But can we create, or even alter, the original standards on which these are based? Can we control the rotation of our planet and its revolutions around the sun? No. Absolute, unchangeable standards for time exist way beyond our grasp.

We can measure distance by using meters, or quantify spaces in volumes and liters, or modify sound using woofers and tweeters. But can we change the distance of our planet from the sun or control the rain that fills our oceans or demolish any trace of sound by using the yardsticks we have constructed? The standards we make end up pointing us to sizes and proportions and levels beyond our comprehension.

And we've become obsessed with establishing standards that will improve our quality of life. We have determined the appropriate shelf life for a can of tuna fish and placed speed limits along our highways. But no matter how many standards we design to enhance life, have we ever been able to create it or bring it back once it has escaped, leaving an empty corpse?

You see, every standard we produce points us to the fact that there must be a Higher Source of standards. Something or Someone beyond us must have formed the very things we are driven to define and control.

WE HAVE AN INTERNAL UNDERSTANDING OF RIGHT AND WRONG

Although we obviously have a very strong internal drive to set standards that will maintain order and help us pursue excellence in the physical areas of our lives, we no longer apply such standards to moral situations. When it comes to Right and Wrong, our culture has decided that there are no rules that apply to every single person, all the time, no matter where they are. We say that each individual is entitled to identify what is good and bad or right and wrong according to his or her own particular set of circumstances. Therefore, deciding the right moral response to a given situation has become very *subjective* (dependent on the situation) and *personal* (defined only by the individuals concerned).

Take honesty, for example. Most of your friends would say that, although it is wrong to lie or cheat or steal *most* of the time, there are some occasions when it is acceptable or even necessary. They would probably agree that it is wrong to lie to a police officer. However, they would argue that it is not only okay, it is sometimes best, to lie if telling the truth could hurt someone emotionally. You would probably be applauded for your sensitivity if you told Sean that it was Kevin who had just called you on the phone — when, in fact, the person you had been talking to for the past half hour was the girl Sean wanted to date. Most teenagers these days do not believe that an *objective, universal* standard for

Right and Wrong exists when it comes to honesty. In other words, they refuse to accept a standard that applies to all people, everywhere, all the time, regardless of the situation.

Jonathan, do you remember when you were in the sixth grade and Granny gave you a gizmo that was a combination calculator, calendar, and note keeper for your birthday? It was a kid-style personal organizer. You loved it! You programmed all kinds of games into it. It even had a feature that allowed you to play games across the room with anyone else who had a similar gizmo. We had to warn you constantly to use it wisely, or we would not allow you to take it to school. For the most part you complied. That gift actually turned out to be a great little device for helping you keep track of assignments and appointments — and friends' telephone numbers.

Your organizer was so neat that other kids constantly asked to borrow it and play with it. But one day someone wanted it so badly that he stole your whole backpack — books, papers, lunch, organizer, and all — in order to get it. The next day the backpack was discovered. It still contained all your books and papers and a rotten ham sandwich, but it was missing the organizer.

Do you remember how you felt when you found out that your organizer was missing? You were hurt and angry. You wanted to beat up whoever had stolen it — and you might have if you had ever found out who it was!

The point I am making is this: when your organizer was stolen, you felt that you had suffered an injustice. You instinctively knew that what had happened to you was *wrong*. Your feelings referenced some moral law that you expected others to abide by — not just yourself. And all your friends felt exactly the same way you did. No one thought that the thief was entitled to his or her own opinion of Right and Wrong based on the circumstances at the time of the heist. You all appealed to a moral law that you believed applied to everyone all the time.

Do you see what I'm getting at? Instinctively there are times when we all judge certain things to be right or certain things to be wrong regardless of the circumstances. The funny thing is that often the only time that we appeal to this objective, universal sense of justice is when we feel that we have been wronged — just as you did when your organizer was stolen.

C. S. Lewis put it this way:

> The most remarkable thing is this. Whenever you find a man who says he does not believe in a real Right and Wrong, you will find that same man going back on this a moment later. He may break his promise to you, but if you try breaking one to him he will be complaining "It's not fair" before you can say Jack Robinson. . . .
>
> It seems, then, we are forced to believe in a real Right and Wrong. People may sometimes be mistaken about them, just as people sometimes get their sums wrong; but they are not a matter of mere taste and opinion any more than the multiplication table.[1]

Whether we're willing to admit it or not, we all agree with Lewis that there are some absolute standards that exist outside of our own abilities to reason. We all apply what he calls "real" Rights and Wrongs to our life situations every day. For instance, regardless of what we think about the circumstances surrounding her actions, we know that it is wrong for a new mother to destroy her newborn child, no matter how distraught she is. Regardless of his motives, we would argue that a man who bombs a building filled with innocent men, women, and children must be punished. We all hold to some truths that are objective and universal and, therefore, absolute.

If we truly believed that the determination of Right and Wrong was up to the individual, we would have done away with our court systems and jails and speeding tickets and all of our other standards for order and decency a long time ago. But we haven't. We know that they are necessary to prevent chaos. So we demand social adherence to certain Rights and Wrongs while hypocritically demanding that other determinations of Right and Wrong are personal and situational.

Because we all seem to turn innately to objective, universal moral standards at certain times in our lives, do you think there could possibly be one set of absolute moral standards — a yardstick that was created outside the limitations of our human minds? One that is not skewed by our preconceived ideas or warped by our improper perspectives? Is there a standard we can go to for answers when our opinions and judgments conflict with someone else's? Could there be a set of standards that applies to all people at all times under all circumstances? If there is, who established this universal set of rules, and where is it defined for us? Listen to what Josh McDowell says in his book *Right from Wrong:*

> It is impossible to arrive at an objective, universal, and constant standard of truth and morality without bringing God onto the stage. If an objective standard of truth and morality exists, it cannot be the product of the human mind (or it will not be objective): it must be the product of another Mind. If a constant and unchanging truth

exists, it must reach beyond human timelines (or it would not be constant); it must be eternal. If a universal rule of right and wrong exists, it must transcend individual experience (or it will not be universal); it must be above us all. Yet, absolute truth must be something — or Someone — that is common to all humanity, to all Creation.

Those things — those requirements for a standard of truth and morality — are found only in one person — God. God is the Source of all truth.[2]

GOD DETERMINES THE STANDARDS FOR RIGHT AND WRONG

We can establish the fact that God exists by making five observations (you might want to refer to Question 1 in my book *Sticking Up for What I Believe*,[3] where each of these is thoroughly discussed):

1. There has to be a *sufficient cause* to verify the existence of the universe. This cause must exist outside of the boundaries of time and space. Otherwise it, too, would have to have a cause. Therefore, it has to be eternal.

2. The fact that our universe is constantly moving and expanding demands an explanation. What or Who caused the first *motion*? Something immobile cannot suddenly move without some kind of shove.

3. The *design* we see in nature (the seasons and tides and life cycles of plants and animals, and so on) implies that there must be a Designer. Design cannot come into existence on its own.

4. The fact that we universally prize qualities such as honesty, wisdom, and courage, and accept that certain char-

acteristics are better than others infers the existence of a standard against which we measure such attributes. The existence of such a universal *morality* points out the existence of an ultimate Good.

5. The universe contains people with personalities — minds and wills and emotions. These could not be the products of an impersonal force, as the effect can never be greater than the cause. *Personality* can only be imparted by a personal being.

Have you hung in there with me? If you have, you will realize that we are left with an eternal, personal, intelligent, ethical God as the only sufficient cause for the existence of the universe and the only possible creator of mankind. Because He is the Designer and Creator and Keeper of the entire universe and all it contains, logically He also must be the origin and foundation of everything we call moral or good. That would mean God is the Maker and Keeper of absolute standards when it comes to morality. *He* is the One who establishes the measurements for all that is Right and Wrong.

If this is true, Right and Wrong are not merely subjective, personal judgments we make depending on our situation. They are not based on our experiences or limited by our weaknesses. They are concrete, objective, universal, indisputable standards based on God's nature and character. But how can we find out what they are?

THE BIBLE DEFINES RIGHT AND WRONG

If you have difficulty accepting the Bible as God's written Word, I would suggest that you read *Sticking Up for What I Believe* Question 3, "How Do We Know That the Bible Is a Reliable Source?" In that chapter we talk about the reliability of the Bible

as a document. Over and over it has proven to be completely cred-
ible when it has been held accountable to historical facts and
archaeological findings. Never has anyone been able to prove that
it contains any false information.

We discussed how impossible it would have been for more
than forty different authors living on three different continents
over a period of 1,500 years to complete one document contain-
ing sixty-six different volumes that conveyed one consistent message. Yet they did! Even when you guys are in the same room at
the same time, the four of you can't agree who left the top off the
bottle of soda or how the toothpaste got smeared all over the
bathroom mirror! There is no way those forty-plus men in such different time frames and under such diverse conditions could have
produced such a harmonious document without some kind of
supernatural help.

In addition, at least one quarter of the Bible was unfulfilled
prophecy at the time it was written. But everything happened, or
is happening, just the way the Bible predicted it would. The
authors had no way of knowing that these events would take place
without the help of a Higher Source.

If you study it carefully, you will realize that there is only one
wise conclusion to make about the Bible — it is the Word of God!
Through it He has chosen to reveal His character. And in it He has
chosen to write out His standards for our behavior.

God is the Originator of all truth. He is the Keeper of all the
yardsticks in the universe. And He conveys His moral standards to
us through the Bible. We can take any behavior and measure it
against His character and His Word to see if it is Right or Wrong.

No, Right and Wrong are not up to the individual! Right and
Wrong are up to God! They are based on God's character, and they
are conveyed to us in the Bible. We cannot live by God's princi-

ples, or comprehend His plans, or enjoy His blessings without reading and understanding His Word. It is the only source of indisputable truth. Just as the yardstick provided a standard that did away with any doubt about whose tower was taller, God's Word shows us His standards so that we are left with no doubts about what is Right and what is Wrong.

In the next few chapters, I want to share God's standards with you. I want you to know why He established them and how they can bring great joy into your life.

SUMMARY

An internal need for standards exists in each individual and in our society as a whole. An intellectual assessment of this need leads us to understand that the ultimate source of all standards lies outside our human capabilities and reason. We also must admit that often, when we are wronged, we appeal to an internal standard of Right and Wrong that is objective and universal.

Absolute standards for Right and Wrong are established by the God who created and keeps the universe. They are not left up to the individual to determine. They are based on God's character and revealed to us in His Word, the Bible. Only by reading it can we know what is truly Right and Wrong. Only by accepting His standards can we enjoy life the way He wants us to.

DILEMMA #2

WHY SHOULD I LIVE A MORAL *Life in Such an Immoral Society?*

WE STILL ROLL OUR EYES AND SHAKE OUR HEADS WHENEVER SOMEONE mentions King, the Boston terrier all four of you bought when you combined your Christmas dollars one year. We all knew the very first time we saw him that he was no ordinary animal. He was a frisky, wriggling ball of enthusiasm and life, and he wriggled his way right into our hearts. Little did we know that his energy and sense of adventure would soon leave us exhausted. (We seem to have an uncanny way of acquiring lively animals!)

King was not a house dog. He made that perfectly clear to us the very first day we brought him home. His goal in life was to rip apart anything he could get his mouth on. In order to accommodate him, we removed most of our patio furniture and gave him full run of our big back porch. But King wasn't satisfied. Even with a lot of romping room and climbing space, the porch was too limited for his satisfaction. We finally decided we had to mend the chain-link fence bordering our property so that King could have full run of the backyard.

However, just a few days after we freed him from the back porch, King tunneled his way under the newly fixed fence and out of the yard. We found him digging up the rose bushes next door. That weekend we buried footers along the entire fence so it would be impossible for him to dig his way out.

But King still managed to make his way to freedom. He was so clever and agile that he actually found a way to climb the chain links on the gate. Then he would remove the pin on the latch with his teeth, push it up with his nose, and swing his way into the outside world! King spent so much time trying to get out of our backyard that he had very little time to explore its exciting nooks and crannies or to play with all of the wonderful toys you guys made and bought for him.

Sometimes King escaped for just a few hours of adventure before we tracked him down and captured him. Other times he would creep back home after several days, in need of both food and sleep. Several times he returned as sick as a dog, obviously having gotten into something that wasn't meant for canine consumption. (I always wondered where we got that phrase before I watched King ralphing in the backyard!) But one time he didn't return at all. I found him lying in the middle of the street. A car had hit him. Although Dr. Tom gave him wonderful care, King was never the same after that accident.

King was oblivious to the harm that waited for him on the other side of our fence. He viewed our backyard as a place of penalty and restriction, when actually it was a place of security. He did not understand that it was designed to protect him. He failed to recognize our love and the value of the limits we had set for him. All we ever wanted to do was protect him and provide for him and play with him. He didn't realize that accepting minimal confinement could have kept him from a lifetime of pain.

Well, the world you face outside our home is every bit as alluring and dangerous as the one King longed for outside our fence. Every day you have to contend with extreme emotional pressures to excel in your schoolwork or to compete on superior levels in extracurricular activities. You are constantly forced to tackle temptations like cheating and dishonesty in your quest for excellence. You are pressured by social demands to maintain certain friendships and keep up specific appearances. You face physical dangers from drunk drivers, distraught classmates, and deadly diseases. And you battle spiritual challenges that mock your upbringing and belittle your beliefs.

There is no way that you, or any other teenager, can survive in the outside world without being harmed in some way. But God has provided a place for you to grow up where you can enjoy real freedom and fun. Because He loves you so much, God has constructed a fence for you — an enclosure — where He can provide for all your needs and protect you from the things that can harm you socially, emotionally, spiritually, and sometimes even physically. This place of security and protection is within the boundaries of His standards for Right and Wrong — the moral standards He has defined in the Bible.

GOD'S STANDARDS SET US FREE

Unfortunately, most of us are a lot like King. Instead of viewing God's laws and commandments as His way of providing for us and protecting us, we see them as restrictions that limit and confine us. We waste most of our time running up and down the fence line — just like King did. We question His placement of the perimeters. We don't realize that the boundaries God has placed around us provide more freedom than we could ever explore in a lifetime. We choose to feel penalized rather than protected. And we look for every chance to escape.

This is exactly what happened to Adam and Eve in the Garden of Eden. God placed them in a paradise more perfect than anything we could ever imagine. The freedom they experienced was unbelievable. They faced no physical dangers. They had no problems in their relationship. They were under no social pressures or standards. There were no deadlines or crises competing for their attention.

There was only one restriction — one little fence! It formed a boundary around a tree that stood in the middle of the most unimaginably magnificent paradise ever created. But it, too, was a part of the freedom that God created for His beloved creatures. You see, in order to be truly free, Adam and Eve had to be given the opportunity to choose to worship and obey God or to reject Him and live in disobedience. If they had not been given such a choice, they would have been merely robots, mechanically and unwillingly obeying a dictator who demanded their allegiance. Adam and Eve were allowed to eat all the food they wanted from lots of delicious plants and fruit-bearing trees, but God asked them not to eat any fruit from that one tree in the middle of their paradise.

You know the rest of the story. Instead of staying away from the tree that was off-limits and enjoying everything else in paradise, Eve stood there longingly eyeing its fruit. It became the focus of her attention, and it didn't take long for her to give in to the temptation to ignore God's standard. And quite easily she convinced Adam to join her. They relied on their own extremely limited wisdom to make a terrible decision.

"Obviously God placed the boundary there because He doesn't really love us," they must have reasoned in order to validate their feelings. "He's just looking for a way to restrict us and limit our pleasure. How could He possibly know what is best for *us*?"

Temporarily blinded to the glorious freedom all around them, they became consumed by the restriction. Instead of finding the freedom they were trying to pursue, they and their children became slaves to stress and corruption and injustice and pain.

In order to restore freedom in the chaos that followed, God instituted new boundaries, or standards. Instead of placing one small fence around one little tree, He had to define many regulations. In a world that became full of sin, He confined His children in a much smaller space in order to protect them and provide for them. But they kept crawling over, under, around, and through His fences and getting into trouble.

Do you remember the part of the Old Testament story where the children of Israel were held captive by the Egyptians for four hundred years and how they were subject to slave labor and suffered under the harsh treatment of the Pharaohs? Well, right after God rescued them and led them across the Red Sea, He sat them down at the base of Mount Sinai so they could catch their breath and so He could teach them a few things about maintaining and enjoying the freedom He had just won for them. Referring to God as *Yahweh* (the name the Israelites used), Vernard Eller explains in his own words what happened when He gave them the Ten Commandments:

> Yahweh is saying in effect: "You are free men, right?"
>
> "Right!"
>
> "And it took me to get you that way, right?"
>
> "Right!"
>
> "I have rather adequately demonstrated that your freedom is my prime concern, right?"
>
> "Right!"
>
> "And having done what I did, I have proved

myself to be the world's leading expert on freedom, right?"

"Right!"

"Fine! Then let old Yahweh give you a few helpful tips on how to be free men and stay that way, OK?"

The negativity of the commandments marks off small areas into which free men ought not go — precisely so that they can remain free to roam anywhere else in the great wide world.[1]

God is the Master of Freedom. Constantly in the Bible we read about Him rescuing people from their bondage and despair. If they had been willing to abide by His standards in the first place, they never would have found themselves in such a mess.

Unfortunately, my generation has failed to learn its lessons from Adam and Eve. We have been very busy over the past few decades tearing down most of the fences that God erected for our protection. We have decided that Right and Wrong are up to the individual. We are adamant that we don't need universal boundaries. Yet in the process of expressing our "freedom", we have become hostages in a world that is sick with sin and immorality — and we have brought you along. What we call "freedom" is costing us so much! We now have to survive in a chaotic world filled with fear, mistrust, and pain.

A long time ago — before any of you were born — Dad and I decided to take tennis lessons. The only time we could do it together was in the morning, so a couple of days a week we got up early and drove to the city courts in Dallas. Because we had the first lessons of the day, we sometimes arrived even before the instructor did. That gave us time to warm up and a chance to volley back and forth for a while. This was a lot of fun, so we decided to get to the courts even earlier so we could have even more volleying time. But sometimes we arrived so early that the nets had not even been suspended.

Some days we played tennis for half an hour before the nets were hung and tightened. This added a whole new dimension to our game. Not being restricted by the height of a net sure increased the length of our volleys! We no longer had to struggle to serve the ball into the opposite court, or worry about burying our backhands into the net.

Because our tennis seemed to be improving so much without the net, we decided it might be even better if we ignored the lines. Of course, without a net or lines and so much open space to cover, we decided it would be okay to let the ball bounce twice before we returned it. With our new rules (or lack of them), a single volley sometimes lasted a full five minutes!

One weekend we decided to watch a tennis tournament at the Civic Center. Among many others, the world's most energetic young tennis player was playing. She was from Australia, and her name was Evonne Goolagong. (I know you've never heard of her, but she was very famous back in the seventies — like I said, this was a *long* time ago.)

That Friday night Evonne really struggled. She kept serving into the net or volleying past the baseline. We wanted to holler to her, "Hey, Evonne, get rid of the net! It's much more fun without it. Forget the lines. You'll do better if you ignore them." But we knew she wouldn't listen to us. She had spent too many years practicing and experiencing the joy of effectively staying within the boundaries of the game to give it up that easily.

About halfway through the match, everything turned around for Evonne. She began to ace her serves. Her baseline strokes were well placed, and her volleys became very efficient. Although

I don't recall the name of her opponent, I do recall having witnessed a very well-played, exciting match, and Evonne ended up winning the whole tournament. That night we realized how beautiful the game of tennis is supposed to be.

You see, without lines, no one can really play tennis. Without a net, no one is free to experience the pleasure the game can bring. This is true in life. Every freedom has a corresponding obligation. Jonathan wouldn't be free to play the guitar if he didn't spend a lot of time practicing strum patterns and learning the chords. None of you could enjoy the game of baseball if you didn't play by its rules and regulations. They each have a purpose. They allow you to enjoy the full potential of the game. Without standards or rules, we can't experience freedom; we can experience only chaos.

Each of the boundaries God has so carefully outlined in His Word, the Bible, also has a purpose, and each one is ultimately designed to bring us real freedom. It is only within the limits of these boundaries that we can experience fulfillment and peace in a world full of sin. It is only when we stay inside them that God promises to protect us and provide for us.

GOD'S STANDARDS PROTECT US

Because He is sovereign, God has a much better grasp of the dangers we face than we ever will. He is totally aware of every detail of every second of our existence in its entire context. Wow, think about that for a few seconds! God knows the whos, whats, whys, wheres, and whens of every aspect of our lives for all eternity.

You have to admit that being privy to that kind of knowledge must give God a pretty good angle on what is best for us. When He tells us we should not lie or steal or cheat or commit sins of lust and sexual immorality, He must have a very good reason. He knows exactly what lies ahead of us if we choose to take those wrong paths. He knows the mental, emotional, and physical pain that accompany each of them. Because He can see ahead, He recognizes that some of the paths we think lead to opportunities for acceptance and advancement actually disguise obstacles that will cause us to stumble and get badly hurt. So He warns us to stay away from them — they are outside the boundaries of His protection. He is also aware that some of the paths we must take in obedience to His standards can be pretty lonely. But He also knows that wonderful, lifetime friends can be waiting just around the next bend if we stay on the path He has chosen. We are so limited in our perspectives. We can see only a small snapshot of what is really taking place. God sees the whole picture.

I have wonderful memories of Zach and MattE playing in the College World Series in Omaha, Nebraska. (Zach competed there as a pitcher for Florida State University for three years, and MattE was the right fielder for two of those years.) I know that neither of you will ever forget the Stanford game — one of the last times you played collegiate ball together. During the fifth inning, the starting pitcher for FSU got in some trouble, and the coach sent for the lefty from the bullpen. That was Zach. Zach had a history of getting the team out of a jam. This time he came in with two men on base and no outs. I kept my eyes closed, my head bowed, and my teeth clenched the whole time he warmed up, wondering if he would be able to do it again.

Somehow Zach managed to pitch the team out of trouble. I let out a huge sigh of relief when that inning was over! As a matter of fact, it was probably the first breath I exhaled in close to ten minutes. But the coach decided to leave Zach in to pitch the next inning . . . and the next . . . and the next. He pitched the rest of the game! I was turning blue from holding my breath and getting ulcers from biting my lips! Every time Zach fell behind in the count, I'd look at the coach, hoping he was planning to take my son out. When a player from the other team smacked a ball through the infield, I wanted to yell, "That's okay, Zach! You've done your job. Let someone else pitch now." When a ball was hit to right field, I'd close my eyes and pray that MattE would catch it.

Well, FSU won the game and Zach was the winning pitcher! It was a glorious moment — one we celebrated for a long time.

Several days after we arrived home, we watched the game on videotape with a friend. This time I smiled and chatted through the whole game. When Zach trotted onto the field in the fifth inning, I grinned and jokingly exclaimed, "Here he comes to save the day!" When Zach got behind in the count, I encouraged him, "That's okay, buddy. Hang in there. You'll get this guy out." When someone smacked a ball through the infield I thought, *Don't worry about it, Zach, he won't get past second base.* When a fly ball was hit to right field, I'd clap ahead of time knowing that MattE was going to make a wonderful catch.

What could possibly have changed my outlook and my attitude so much? It was exactly the same game I had watched with so much anxiety in Omaha! Of course, the difference was that I had already seen the ninth inning. I had been there, and I knew the outcome. I knew that Zach had done a super job, that MattE had caught the ball whenever it was hit to him, and that their team had won.

Well, God has already seen our ninth inning! He knows exactly what is going to happen to us for the rest of our lives. He knows exactly what trials and temptations we will face along the way and exactly the best way to get us where He knows we need to be. He has created standards that will protect us in every situation. If we live according to His standards, we will be blessed. But if we don't, His protection and blessing cannot accompany us.

For just one moment, think about the fact that God *knows* every single detail of your life. Then add to that the truth that He is *powerful* enough to change any feature of your life that He desires. Then attach the reality that He *loves* you so much that He will only ever do what is absolutely the very best for you. You are left with a *very* good reason to live a moral life as defined by His standards. If you can really grasp these three qualities of God's character, you will *never* ever doubt *any* of the standards He has made clear in the Bible:

1. *God is omniscient.* He knows every detail of every second of everything that will ever happen to you. Matthew 10:30 tells us that He is aware of every single hair that is on your head. (And He knows exactly how many fell out this morning when you were blow-drying!)

2. *God is omnipotent.* He has the power to change anything and everything that is taking place in your life. Ephesians 1:18-20 tells us that the power that raised Jesus Christ from the dead is available for *our* lives. Wow! That means that unless you have a need that is more earth-shattering than being raised from the dead (I can't imagine what that would be), God is quite capable of handling it in your life!

3. *God is love.* He loves you more than anyone on earth ever could or will. According to 1 John 4:16, God *is* love. There is not one speck of His nature that is not loving, nor could He ever take a single action that is not motivated by love. Therefore God can be counted on to always do whatever is the very best for you.

The standards God has designed for us to live by were created on the basis of these three qualities of His character — His omniscience, His omnipotence, and His love. They are designed not only for our good, but for our *best*. They are intended to help us find and enjoy the freedom we seek so intensely.

GOD'S STANDARDS PROVIDE FOR US

Jeremiah 29:11 says, "'For I know the plans that I have for you,' declares the LORD, 'plans to prosper you and not to harm you, plans to give you hope and a future.'" God's standards not only protect us, they provide a safe place where we can prosper. God wants us to enjoy our time here on earth completely. He doesn't say things like "unless you are married, you are not allowed to have sex, no matter how much you love a person," in order to rob us of pleasure. He wants us to hold off until marriage so that we can experience the ultimate pleasure that sex can provide. (We'll talk about that more in Dilemma #5.)

Our obedience to God's standards is not an end in itself. It is a pathway to what is best. It is the route that leads us to a special relationship with God, a place where He can pour out His fabulous blessings in our lives.

Hour after hour, one of your Sunday school teachers worked on a huge contraption in his carport. For more than two years he labored long and hard following step-by-step instructions in a manual. He obeyed each command one at a time until he had built an entire airplane! While other adults were out playing golf or hunting and fishing, he was under his carport working. He didn't follow those instructions just because they were there; or because his wife told him he had to because he had already spent so much money on the kit; or just because he wanted to see if he was capable of following them. He obeyed them because he knew that if he did, in the long run, he could have great pleasure. And he was kind enough to share that pleasure with you. I'll never forget the feeling of panic and delight I experienced as he buzzed over our house with one of you guys seated in the cockpit of his homemade airplane. All the time he spent following directions freed him to enjoy pleasures in life that very few experience!

God is the source of all that is truly good in this world, and He wants to share it with us. He not only owns all the cattle on a thousand hills (Psalm 50:10), He owns all the hills as well (Psalm 95:4). He has so many blessings He wants to give us!

First Corinthians 2:9 tells us, "No eye has seen, no ear has heard, no mind has conceived what God has prepared for those who love him." We can't even begin to comprehend what He has in store for us if we live according to His standards!

SUMMARY

Because He loves us so much, God has constructed a fence for us — an enclosure — where He can provide for all our needs and protect us from anything that could harm us socially, emotionally, spiritually, and physically. This place of security and protection is inside the boundaries of His standards for Right and Wrong, the standards of morality He has defined in the Bible.

Living according to God's standards often frees us from disease, despair, and disappointment that would otherwise follow. It helps us to love completely, to live contentedly, and to enjoy life unashamedly. God's standards provide the basis for great freedom, pleasure, protection, and blessings we can't even imagine in our lives.

DILEMMA #3

HOW CAN I LIVE A MORAL LIFE *in Such an Immoral Society?*

THE ANSWER TO THIS QUESTION IS VERY SIMPLE. YOU CAN'T!

I'm guessing, because you turned the page, that you'd like a more involved explanation. Well, actually, the point isn't that you **can't** live a moral life in such an immoral society. It's that **you** can't live a moral life in such an immoral society — at least, not on your own.

The society we live in blatantly denies the existence of the God who created it. It would rather pursue a life of personal pleasure than live up to the standards of an all-knowing, all-powerful, all-loving God. This is obvious in the music it offers. It is expected in the movies it provides. And it is deliberate in the television programs it produces. Even your public school curriculum often presents its material from a worldview that is godless and has no moral basis. Left on our own to live according to God's standards in this world, none of us would last any longer than a lonely wildebeest in the African wilds. So why does God leave us here — and how can we survive?

THE PROBLEM: WE LIVE IN A WORLD FULL OF WEEDS

Back in my high school days, I had a field hockey coach who took a rather unique approach to establishing her team. On the first day of sign-ups about ninety other girls and I showed up for orientation. To our surprise the new coach informed us that she was not going to make any cuts. Nobody, no matter how untalented or unathletic, would be asked to leave the team. There would be some penalties for lateness or laziness, but nobody would be dismissed, even if they were uncooperative or cantankerous. Noticing the puzzled expressions on our faces, she quickly added, "Don't worry, everyone on the team will be given plenty of playing time."

Her promise seemed ridiculous, as so many girls obviously wanted to play, and it takes only eleven players to field a team. But just a few minutes into the first practice, about one third of the girls laid their hockey sticks down on the grass and walked off the field. They quit the team as soon as the coach announced that we were going to warm up for practice every day by running twelve laps around the hockey field!

"That's nothing," she insisted as the rest of us lay panting on the grass after our three-mile run. "By the end of the season you'll be running twelve miles!" Immediately another third packed up their gym bags and headed home.

The first few practices took every ounce of strength and energy the remaining thirty-one of us could muster as we completed our running, practiced our drills, and learned the game of field hockey for three hours every afternoon after school. We were all so stiff and sore we could hardly walk!

Several of the returning players began to complain. They couldn't understand why the coach didn't just get rid of some of the newer, less talented girls (like me) who made everyone have to do the drills over and over until we got them right. They didn't think it was fair that they had to practice side by side with lousy players and be penalized for their errors.

But by the end of the first two weeks, only about sixteen girls — most of whom were in some kind of decent athletic shape, had at least a little athletic ability, or possessed a tremendous zeal to play field hockey — showed up for practice. It was then that the coach explained her philosophy of establishing a team. She had allowed us to "weed ourselves out." She had not wanted to mistake a true competitor for one of the "weeds" before that player was given a chance to prove herself.

In her office, the coach kept a list of the best players she had coached over the years. None of them had exhibited any apparent skills when she first met them. But because they were dedicated, hard workers and because they were given extra time to develop, they had blossomed into great players. (Believe it or not, by the end of my high school career, I think she had added me to that list.)

According to Matthew 13:24-30, we are living in a world full of weeds. Good people and bad people are playing the game of life side by side every day. Listen to the parable Jesus tells:

> "The kingdom of heaven is like a man who sowed good seed in his field. But while everyone was sleeping, his enemy came and sowed weeds among the wheat, and went away. When the wheat sprouted and formed heads, then the weeds also appeared.
>
> "The owner's servants came to him and said, 'Sir, didn't you sow good seed in your field? Where then did the weeds come from?'
>
> "'An enemy did this,' he replied.
>
> "The servants asked him, 'Do you want us to go and pull them up?'
>
> "'No,' he answered, 'because while you are pulling the weeds, you may root up the wheat with them. Let both grow together until the harvest. At that time I will tell the harvesters: First collect the weeds and tie them in bundles to be burned, then gather the wheat and bring it into my barn.'"

The world is God's wheat field. On His farm, He allows the good and the bad (the wheat and the weeds) to grow alongside each other. This makes life a little rough for the wheat some-times, but God has a reason for allowing the weeds to remain — the Lord of the harvest knows that some of the plants that look like weeds will actually turn out to be wonderful, healthy stalks of wheat.

There are many examples of this taking place in the Bible. Rahab, the harlot, who once was a ragged, risqué weed, put her faith in the God of the Israelites, and she saved the lives of two Israeli spies (Joshua 2). She blossomed beautifully and became a sturdy shoot in the ancestral line of Jesus (Matthew 1:5)!

Saul of Tarsus, who was a poisonous weed at one time, persecuted and killed off all the wheat he could lay his hands on until he was converted on the road to Damascus (Acts 9:1-19). Then he became a staunch stalk of wheat accepting all kinds of hardship and persecution at the hands of other weeds.

If God had chosen to whack all the weeds prior to Rahab's acknowledgment of His existence, or Paul's conversion to Christianity, or your acceptance of Christ's sacrifice on the cross, there would have been a whole lot less wheat at harvest time. To use the analogy of my field hockey team, many of the people who became God's best players would have been cut from the team.

One of the main tasks we have as believers is to help people who look like weeds discover that they, too, can become wheat. We can't do this if we are planted in separate fields. In God's cultivation process, proximity is a necessary part of the process.

This can create a problem for the wheat if we allow the weeds to take over. We need help in order to remain healthy. We must find ways to raise our stalks of wheat above the weeds so that we can soak in the sunshine. We must dig our roots down firmly into the soil so that we will not be easily uprooted. God provides several resources that will give us the strength and power we need to stand strong and tall and beautiful until harvest time. We must take advantage of them.

GOD'S SOLUTIONS

1. God sends us the Holy Spirit.

A little girl used to invite Matthew to her house to play quite often when they were both preschoolers. She was just as full of energy as he was — and she had wonderful toys! One of Matthew's favorites was a little pink vacuum. He would push that thing all over her house for hours. As the wheels turned, they rubbed against metal plates, making a noise that sounded like a motor. It revved louder and louder the faster it was pushed. In addition to that, this wonderful little vacuum shot bubbles into the air whenever its canister was filled with soapy water.

Matthew loved that toy. Not only was it fun, but he really believed he was accomplishing something worthwhile whenever he "vacuumed" the rug. Then one day he deliberately placed some crumbs and bits of paper in its path. The vacuum failed to pick them up. Matthew became very annoyed with the make-believe machine and moved on to other toys.

Even though he had thought he was doing real work when he pushed that play vacuum, Matthew never actually achieved anything worthwhile. That's because the toy didn't have a motor. As much as it looked and sounded like a real vacuum, without a power mechanism it couldn't accomplish a thing.

The Bible explains that the Holy Spirit is like a motor in our lives. When we accept Jesus Christ as our Savior, He automatically comes to live inside us (see 1 Corinthians 3:16; Galatians 4:6). He provides the power and strength that we do not have on our own to live lives pleasing to God. Anyone who has a relationship with God through Jesus Christ has the Holy Spirit living inside — convicting them of wrong and convincing them of right (see John 16:8,13). It is His job to guide us. It is His desire to make our lives beautiful and productive by filling them with love, joy, peace, patience, kindness, goodness, faithfulness, gentleness, and self-control (see Galatians 5:22-23).

Trying to live a moral life on our own in this immoral world is every bit as futile as trying to vacuum the living room with a little, pink, bubble-blowing vacuum that has no motor. We can't do it without the help of the Holy Spirit.

2. God asks us to pray.

But having a motor inside us is not enough. A little pink vacuum with a little pink motor will pick up no more crumbs or paper than one without a motor — unless it is plugged into a power source. And the way we appropriate the power made available to us by the Holy Spirit is through prayer.

It would be really dumb to try to vacuum an entire house without ever connecting the cleaner to its power source, but I did something almost as bad not long ago! The main hose on my Hoover popped out of its clamp, and I didn't realize it. I did notice that my efforts weren't accomplishing very much, but I continued to vacuum. It wasn't until I was almost finished that I realized the problem. Although it appeared to be in place, the head of the cleaner was totally disconnected from the sucking source.

It's amazing how many Christians are wandering around on this planet with powerful motors inside them — but they're accomplishing nothing. Their motors are disconnected from the source of power. You see, prayer is the cord that hooks up our motor (the Holy Spirit) with God's awesome power.

I'd like to tell you that I understand how prayer works. But I can't. I don't understand why an omniscient, omnipresent, sovereign God who knows every aspect of the entire universe wants me to fill Him in on all the details of my life. But He does!

I can't explain how my desires and my plans and my future can be of importance to Him. But they are!

I don't get why my praise and thanks mean anything to God when zillions of angels stand around His throne singing "glory in the highest" to Him all day long. But they do!

For some reason God has chosen to make prayer the key that unlocks the huge storehouses of heaven and unleashes the power of the Holy Spirit. And He has given that key to us! If we could ever comprehend this completely we would never stop praying.

Prayer is what keeps wheat from being overtaken by weeds. We don't have to comprehend it. We just have to do it!

3. God gives us the Bible.

The principles we need to live by — God's moral standards — are written and explained to us in the Bible. But the fact that they are recorded in a book does us absolutely no good if that book is left sitting on a shelf beside our bed or in the backseat of the family van. We must choose to interact with God's Word.

The same principle applies when taking a shower. The fact that you have a bathroom that includes a showerhead and running water does not guarantee that you will be clean. As a matter of fact, you can turn on the water and leave it running all evening and still be just as filthy when you go to bed as you were when you got home from baseball practice. At some point you have to get your body into that water! Although the water (as well as a little soap and elbow grease) is responsible for washing away the dirt, you have a role to play. You must choose to take advantage of its purpose and participate in its power.

If we truly desire to live a life of wisdom and power among the weeds, we must spend time every day reading and studying the instruction manual God has provided. We must learn ahead of time — *before* we are faced with a moral dilemma — what standards He expects us to live by. If we aren't aware of God's principles and are uncertain of our position, we are likely to make wrong, weedlike choices. We must consistently look to the Bible for guidance. We must search it for solutions to every dilemma that we face. The Bible contains all the directions and answers we will ever need to live lives of moral uprightness in a morally bankrupt world.

4. God expects us to hang around other believers.

We have watched several National Geographic specials together. One of them showed a large herd of wildebeests at their watering hole on the African Serengeti, being stalked by a pride of hungry lions. Frantically, the herd tightened its circumference and steered its young to the center. But off to the side, one lone female kept trailing along on her own. She was either unable or uninterested in staying up with the others. Sure enough, the lions pounced on the opportunity, and soon three sleek-bodied, hunger-driven lions were chasing a frightened wildebeest all over the African terrain. Because she did not hook up with the herd, she allowed herself to become an easy target and a tasty snack.

Unless we surround ourselves with others who adhere to the same biblical standards and accept the same principles that we do, we, too, will become easy prey. We will swiftly and easily be gobbled up by the society around us. To try to stand alone is to invite attack. Christianity was never designed to be a do-it-yourself proposition. The Bible says, "And let us consider how we may spur one another on toward love and good deeds. Let us not give up meeting together, as some are in the habit of doing, but let us encourage one another" (Hebrews 10:24-25). We need others in our lives who will encourage and inspire us to make godly choices, who will hold us accountable for the choices we make, and who will lift us up when we fall.

5. God wants us to maintain an attitude of joy.

Nehemiah 8:10 says, "The joy of the Lord is (our) strength." Living a moral life according to God's standards in an immoral society is not an easy assignment. But growing into strong stalks of wheat requires rain as well as sunshine. Even when things are tough, we can still experience God's joy. We can know that He is aware of every detail concerning our circumstances. We can trust that He is powerful enough to change any detail of the situation if He wants. And we can relax and release our tensions, knowing that He loves us enough to do only what is very best for us.

First Thessalonians 5:18 says, "Give thanks in all circumstances, for this is God's will for you in Christ Jesus." Is it really possible to give thanks in *all* situations? It is, if we believe Romans 8:28: "And we know that in *all* things God works for the good of those who love him, who have been called according to his purpose" (emphasis added).

God knows the perfect quantity of sunshine, and He allows precisely the right amount of rain to fall in our lives for us to grow into fruitful stalks of wheat that will provide a worthwhile harvest. Learning to trust Him results in joy. That joy gives us the desire and courage to live according to the standards God has given us.

SUMMARY

Living a moral life in an immoral world is like trying to become a sturdy stalk of wheat in a world full of weeds. (We must not forget that we were once considered weeds ourselves.) If we experience the power of the Holy Spirit in our lives and allow it to be put into action through the practice of prayer; if we desire to know the standards God has established for us in the Bible and gain strength from the encouragement and help of other believers; if we trust God's leading in our lives and experience the relaxation and joy that this confidence brings; then we will be able to live a moral life in an immoral society.

DILEMMA #4

EXACTLY HOW HONEST AM I Supposed to Be?

HALIMA WAS A WORKING WOMAN. BUT SHE DID NOT PUT IN AN ORDINARY forty-hour workweek in an everyday office. She sweated through backbreaking labor in dusty fields, from dawn till dusk, seven days a week. The pressure of working, raising children, and trying to maintain some kind of home life was heavy, especially as she found herself in a nomadic society that offered very few conveniences and even fewer rights for its women.

I was very young when I first met Halima. She was — well, I'm not exactly sure how old she was. Let's just say that from the looks of her gnarled fingers and wrinkled brow, she was "well worn." She was from a Fulani tribe in West Africa that herded its cattle through the "bush country" near where my dad ran his leprosy clinics.

Every week I watched as Halima came down the long, dusty path that led to our kitchen door. Her walk was tall and smooth, almost elegant. Her hips swayed rhythmically back and forth as her bare feet kicked up a little cloud of dust along the sandy trail. Her neck and head were ramrod straight, and a huge gourd filled with milk rode steadily on top.

As Halima approached, she became even more fascinating. The sun flashed off her bright fingernails, dyed red from many hours spent soaking in berry juices. She wore large tin hoops in her ears and she had a wide, toothless grin. I always smiled "real big" at Halima so that she would have to smile back. That way I could see if she had any new gaps where she used to have teeth. I worried about how she would eat if she lost any more.

When she arrived, Halima would sit on her haunches, chewing on bark with her few remaining teeth, while my mother measured the milk and sent it into the kitchen to be strained and boiled. I sat watching from my swing that hung low from the nearby mango tree. Halima would thank my mother for her generous payment (a few tin cans as well as a few round shillings), then she would head back down the lonely dirt path.

Over time my mother began to suspect that something was wrong with the milk. It seemed thinner than usual. Was Halima doctoring it — watering it down in order to get a few more shillings for her hard labor and her long walk? One day my mother asked her.

"No! No!" Halima protested in her native tongue. "Halima would never do that. It must be the cows. They are weak. The sun is too strong. The grass is too sparse. There is only thin milk to sell. It is all the cows have to offer!"

But the evidence proved her wrong. A few days later, three tiny polliwogs were swimming in the middle of the straining cloth. Just as my mother had suspected, Halima had been stopping at a pond on her way to our house for months. There she had filled her gourd to the top with tepid water. She had carefully tried to remove any evidence. But that day, little eggs had slipped in unnoticed and hatched as she completed her journey to our house.

That was the last time I remember seeing Halima and her toothless grin. She had cheated. Then she had lied. She had been caught. Now she was gone.

I wondered who would buy her milk. Who would watch for her down the long, winding paths of her life? Who would care about her teeth?

I soon forgot about Halima. There were plenty of other interesting characters more than happy to sell us milk. But I'll always remember the lesson she taught me. No matter what the pressures are, or how easy or justifiable it seems, cheating is never worth it. Sooner or later you get caught, because sooner or later there are bound to be polliwogs flip-flopping in some-one's straining cloth.

Halima saw dishonesty as a solution to the many problems she was facing in life. The grass was thin, the rains had not come, and her cows were not producing enough milk for her to earn a living. By cheating and adding water to the milk, she realized she could cut down on her incredible workload and increase her meager profits. Besides, as we later found out, most of the other "milk women" had been doing it for a long time.

Once she made the decision to cheat, the deceit seemed to pay off — at least for a little while. However, when her fraud was discovered, Halima was trapped. She compounded her dishonesty by lying to my mother. Instead of providing a simple solution to a real problem, dishonesty became a complex, compounding disaster. Halima was left with no place to sell her milk.

Dishonesty knows no cultural, ethnic, or financial boundaries. Lying, cheating, and stealing take place anywhere human beings live and compete. Dishonesty seems to provide an easy way to get ahead, an avenue to impress others, an opportunity to gain approval.

WHAT IS GOD'S STANDARD FOR HONESTY?

God is a God of integrity and truth. According to Titus 1:2 and Hebrews 6:18, He is a God who does not lie. Deuteronomy 32:4 describes His character this way: "His works are perfect, and all his ways are just. A faithful God who does no wrong, upright and just is he." Anything contrary to God's nature is wrong. Therefore lying, stealing, cheating, deceiving, and dishonesty *in any form* are completely sinful and immoral.

God not only reveals His standards for integrity through His character, but He explains them very clearly to us in the Bible. Two of the Ten Commandments deal with honesty. We must never steal (see Exodus 20:15) or bear false witness against our neighbors (see 20:16). Leviticus puts it even more plainly: "Do not steal. Do not lie. Do not deceive one another" (19:11). And the next few verses in the chapter command us not to cheat others out of what is rightfully theirs.

God's expectations are black and white. Proverbs 12:22 says that God "detests lying lips, but he delights in men who are truthful."

His principles regarding integrity are clearly stated in the New Testament as well. Ephesians 4:25 says, "Therefore each of you must put off falsehood and speak truthfully to his neighbor." Titus 2:10 prohibits stealing and promotes trustworthiness.

Based on God's character and His commands, it is unquestionably clear what God's views are when it comes to integrity. Complete honesty is His standard for all people everywhere, all the time. Any form of dishonesty is sin.

WHY DID GOD DESIGN THIS STANDARD?

This criterion of "complete honesty" is not a random standard that God invented just to see if He could trip us up. No, as with all His standards, God established it for our protection and our freedom.

He knew that if we obeyed it, our lives would be so much better off than if we didn't.

I vividly recall an incident that took place many years ago (many more than I would like to acknowledge!). I was sitting in my seventh-grade English class, working on an assignment. It was the last period of the day, and we knew that in a few minutes we would be dismissed to attend a pep rally for the basketball team. Meanwhile we kept quietly busy as the teacher wandered up and down the rows, helping us with our papers.

Unexpectedly, there was a knock on the door and the teacher was asked to step out into the hallway. As she did, she turned and spoke emphatically to us. "I don't want any talking at all! I don't want you to leave your seats for any reason. You must work on your own."

Then she closed the door behind her.

Her directions were clear and concise, and there was no reason for any of us not to comprehend them completely. However, two minutes after she left, the room was in chaos as kids ran from desk to desk swapping papers and visiting friends. Most of the students who did not leave their seats were engaged in conversations with classmates surrounding them.

Because I knew that what I didn't finish in class I would have to complete at home, I spent most of my time working on my assignment. But occasionally I turned around to ask a question or make a comment to my friend who sat behind me.

Suddenly, the door flew open and in walked the teacher, noticeably perturbed with our behavior. Students dashed madly to their seats, and the room immediately hushed.

"All right," she stated quietly, after staring at us for what seemed like an hour. "I want everyone who kept their mouths shut and did not leave their seats while I was out of the room to stand up. The rest of you remain seated."

Three of the twenty-eight students slowly rose to their feet.

What's this? I thought to myself as I looked around the room. *I know for a fact that all three of those kids talked a lot more than I did—and Patricia even left her seat! This just isn't fair!*

It only took a split second for me to rationalize everything in my brain. Obviously, it was only right for me to be included with the good kids, because I had behaved much more honorably than any of them had. So I quickly hopped to my feet.

"Okay, the four of you will get A's for this assignment. You don't need to turn it in," the teacher explained. "Now you may leave and go to the pep rally. The rest of you will stay here and work on the assignment."

As I turned to pick up my belongings I noticed a strange look on my friend's face — a mixture of bewilderment, hurt, and anger. She had remained seated when the good kids were asked to stand, even though she had never left her seat and had hardly spoken when the teacher was out of the room.

Needless to say, I did not enjoy that pep rally. I felt miserable knowing that I had lied and that my friend had been brave enough to tell the truth. She didn't speak to me the rest of that week. As a matter of fact, my lack of honesty tainted our friendship for quite a while.

1. Honesty protects our relationships by providing a basis of trust.

God knew that dishonesty would destroy friendships. Once the thin thread of trust is broken in a relationship, it is very hard to tie it back together. When people realize that you are willing to lie, regardless of the reason, they find it much harder to trust you.

"But I would never lie to my friends," you might insist. If they know that you are willing to lie to others, how can they ever be completely sure that you won't lie to them? But on the flip side, if they see you standing up for what is true and honest even when it is very difficult, they will know that you can always be trusted.

Josh McDowell put it this way: "If you tell the truth all the time, I can believe you all the time. But if you only tell the truth some of the time, I can't believe you any of the time."[1] Honesty protects our friendships by providing a basis of trust.

2. Honesty protects us from guilt and gives us peace of mind.

Dishonesty robs us of peace and fills us with guilt — and guilt is a heavy burden to carry. David knew its weight. In Psalm 38:4 he wrote, "My guilt has overwhelmed me like a burden too heavy to bear." Once again, listen to what McDowell has to say: "Guilt is among the most powerful emotions, and it will cling to the dishonest heart like a python, choking the life out of its victim."[2]

Guilt takes away any sense of joy, fulfillment, or enthusiasm that we might have experienced if we had handled the situation with integrity. As a matter of fact, we are more likely to doubt ourselves and question our abilities if we cheated or lied our way to success. *Could I have accomplished this if I had not been dishonest?* The question will haunt us if we relied on deceit to get us through.

It is impossible to approach God properly if we have a guilty conscience. Just as Adam and Eve hid from God in the Garden of Eden after their disobedience, we no longer feel the freedom to enjoy God's company when we have been deceitful or dishonest.

Psalm 15:1 asks the question, "LORD, who may dwell in your sanctuary? Who may live on your holy hill?" In other words, "God, who can enjoy the privilege of being in your presence?" Verse 2 answers it this way, "He whose walk is blameless and who does what is righteous, who speaks the truth from his heart."

Our consciences were designed to prevent us from enjoying the results of our deceitful efforts. However, let me warn you, it is possible for us to dull our consciences and cause them to betray us. First Timothy 4:2 warns against deceitful teachings that "come through hypocritical liars, whose consciences have been seared as with a hot iron."

I remember a story I heard a long time ago about an American Indian chief who described his conscience as a triangle with three sharp edges. He explained that the triangle revolved in his heart whenever he did something wrong. Round and round it went, pricking and gouging him until he made the situation right. "But," he added to his explanation, "if I let it keep turning for too long, the edges wear off, and I don't feel the pain anymore. That's when I get in really big trouble."

God gave each of us a conscience for a specific reason — to alert us when we are in violation of His standards. We cannot afford to ignore its warnings.

3. Honesty protects us from humiliation and gives us a sense of fulfillment.

Dishonesty can easily lead us into further violations of God's standards. It is often compounded as we try to rationalize or justify a previous deceitful action. Very quickly a whole web of deceit and dishonesty can be woven in and around and through our lives. Complete honesty protects us from the disgrace that occurs whenever such deception is discovered or dishonesty is revealed. And it cannot remain hidden for long. As the Bible says, "You may be sure that your sin will find you out" (Numbers 32:23).

During the first century, Ananias and Sapphira set out to do a wonderful thing. Acts 5 tells the story of how they sold a piece of property and decided to give some of the money to the new church that had just started in Jerusalem. But because they were seeking the approval of their peers more than the pleasure of honoring God, they decided to lie. They told the church leaders that they had given them *all* of the money they had made on the sale of their property when in fact they had kept some of it for themselves.

What started out as an honorable, praiseworthy deed turned out to be the death of Ananias and Sapphira — literally! (You can read about it in Acts 5:1-11.) They thought they could get away with a lie. But God used their obvious deceit as a lesson to others who might have been tempted to follow their example. Right then and there, He removed them from any further harmful influence. They both dropped dead! Talk about utter humiliation! For two thousand years, they have been known as swindlers who tried to deceive both God and the leaders of the early Christian church.

Honesty removes any possibility of the humiliation and shame inevitably attached to dishonesty. It frees us to experience real accomplishment instead of false, fleeting pride. Proverbs 21:6 says that any "fortune made by a lying tongue is a fleeting vapor and a deadly snare."

Dishonesty always leaves victims in its wake. It defrauds those who are cheated out of something by taking what is rightfully theirs. And it deprives the guilty ones by removing God's blessing from their lives.

In Luke 16, after teaching a lesson about how we should handle our affairs wisely, Jesus concludes by saying, "Whoever can be trusted with very little can also be trusted with much, and whoever is dishonest with very little will also be dishonest with much" (verse 10). If God can't trust you, He isn't going to use you, and therefore you can't experience His blessing.

Stuffing hotel towels into a suitcase or not returning extra change to a sales cashier violates God's standard of honesty just as much as robbing a bank does. A "little white lie" breaks God's law every bit as much as a huge political cover-up. The consequences may be different, but the verdict is still "guilty."

WHY IS IT SO HARD TO ACCEPT THIS STANDARD?

Many of your friends have adopted lifestyles of deceit and dishonesty. They believe that cheating on tests and lying about actions is necessary in order to compete in the ballgame of life. They have accepted lying as a survival skill in a highly competitive world. Dishonesty has become so prevalent that it is often treated as normal. But that doesn't make it right.

Every time Jonathan walked into his sophomore chemistry class last year to take an exam, he knew that more than half the students had already seen the test and gotten the answers from friends who had previously taken it. This provided a real dilemma for him. He knew that his teacher graded the tests on a curve. He was fairly certain that he could not live up to the high end of the curve that would be established by the cheaters. So how could he possibly keep up with the class average and get a good grade? And, because this went on in many of his other classes, how could he expect to get into a good college unless he cheated too? Having to live according to God's standard of honesty seemed very unfair.

Yet, if God is truly God, He must be the God of *everything*. Can you even begin to comprehend that statement? If God is the Keeper of the universe, as we discovered He is in chapter 1, then He is in sovereign control over every aspect of our lives. He is the ultimate Decider of who gets into which college. He is the ultimate Planner of our futures, the ultimate Promoter of our careers, the ultimate Provider of our peace. Our future is not decided nor can it be derailed by the deceit and dishonesty of others.

Jonathan chose not to cheat. This meant he had to study extra hard and pay very close attention every class period while most of his classmates goofed off. Even so, he probably did not get the grades he deserved in his chemistry and math classes. But he did have a peace about his actions and pride in his own accomplishments. (I'm proud of you too, Jonathan, and I know God has special things planned for you because you chose to live according to His standards.)

Remember, God knows every detail of your life. He has the power to change any detail. And He loves you enough to do what's very best. He has established a standard of complete honesty and integrity that He has never revoked. If He looked down from heaven right now and saw just one person walking down the path marked "Honesty," that's the person He would choose to honor and bless. God will use you if He knows He can trust you.

How can you live up to God's standard?

You must make a commitment to hold onto absolute integrity in every detail, in every situation, no matter how big or small. And you must make this commitment before you are faced with a dilemma.

During the course of a day, you are going to have to make dozens of decisions that will test your obedience to God's standard of complete honesty. If you have to decide how to respond each time you are faced with a dilemma, you are going to be much more vulnerable to violating God's standard. You will expend a lot of unnecessary energy; you will constantly subject yourself to the pressure of less honorable peers; and you will fall prey to the recklessness of hasty decision making.

But if you decide ahead of time — once and for all — that you are going to abide by God's standard of complete honesty, you will remove a lot of pressure from your life — and receive a lot of blessings from God!

You must determine that you will not cheat, no matter how many others are doing it to get ahead, nor how much it will affect your grades.

You must make your mind up that you will not lie to get out of a sticky situation, no matter how easy it would be to get away with it.

You must establish ahead of time that you will not steal just to fit in with the crowd — even if it's just a pack of gum and you know that the store manager will never miss it.

You must decide that you will not use your words or actions to deceive anyone for any reason.

Yes, you must commit yourself to the fact that you are going to live a life of complete honesty and integrity regardless of the circumstances. And when you make a bad decision (which on occasion you will), you must not compound it by trying to cover it up. Most people — especially your parents and teachers — are more willing to "forgive and forget" when you admit your mistakes or confess a disobedience than they are to "forgive and forget" an outright lie. We know you are not perfect, and we realize that you need to grow.

SUMMARY

Any form of dishonesty (whether lying, stealing, cheating, or deceiving) violates the standard set by God's character and clearly defined for us in His Word. God did not set a standard of absolute integrity in order to catch us in sin. No, He established it to protect us and provide for us. God wants us to enjoy our lives in every way. Honesty protects our relationships by maintaining a basis of trust. It keeps us from having to carry a burden of guilt, and it gives us peace of mind. It guards us from humiliation and allows us to experience real joy and fulfillment in what we accomplish. God established a standard of complete honesty in order to free us to enjoy all the wonderful blessings and honor that He has prepared for those who obey Him.

It is important to make a concrete decision to be completely honest *before* you are faced with a dilemma involving your integrity. You must decide ahead of time that you are going to abide by God's standards regardless of the circumstances and the pressure from your peers. This will keep you from making unwise, hasty decisions that lead to sin.

DILEMMA #5

WHAT ABOUT SEX — HOW FAR Is Too Far?

A FEW MONTHS AGO I RECEIVED A GIFT IN THE MAIL — A SPECIAL COUPON from one of my favorite clothing stores. There was a silver "scratch-off" square in the middle of the coupon. The instructions said that it could be scratched off at the time of purchase to reveal a certain percentage that would be deducted from the sale. The savings could be anywhere from thirty to fifty percent off the original price.

I was really excited about the gift because I needed a new pair of slacks. Eagerly I scratched off the square to see how much I was going to save. Fifty percent! I was elated. I could save fifty percent on whatever I purchased. I was going to be able to get a really nice pair of slacks.

Then I reread the instructions. Uh-oh. I had goofed up big-time. The instructions clearly stated that the square was to be scratched off "at the time of purchase." I had previously read this restriction, but somehow in my excitement I had ignored it.

I quickly read the tiny print trying to figure out if there was any way to revalidate my coupon. But to no avail. I was angry at myself for being so foolish, but I also found myself becoming very upset with the store for being so narrow-minded. What difference did it make if I scratched their silly coupon off at home or in the store? A 50-percent discount should be a 50-percent discount regardless of where it's discovered!

What was designed to bring me pleasure instead brought me great frustration. But the worst part was that it was my fault. I had disregarded the rules and invalidated my wonderful gift by using it before I was supposed to. I did buy a pair of slacks that day, but they were worth a lot less than the ones I could have bought if I had not used my coupon incorrectly.

Sex is a lot like that coupon. God designed and distributed it as a special gift. He intended for it to be one of the most delightful, fulfilling elements that a human relationship could ever contain. Because God loves us so much, He wants us to enjoy our sexuality completely. He doesn't want us to miss out on any of its beauty or benefits, or have to settle for a cheaper version. And, just as my 50-percent-off coupon came with rules and regulations I had to follow if I wanted to enjoy the benefits it had to offer, God has given us instructions that we must follow if we are going to experience the full magnificence of our fabulous gift. To use it outside these parameters (boundaries) invalidates the tremendous joy that it can bring.

WHAT IS GOD'S STANDARD FOR SEXUAL RELATIONSHIPS?

First John 3:3 tells us that God is pure. Habakkuk 1:13 defines that purity, telling us that His "eyes are too pure to look on evil" and that He "cannot tolerate wrong." Remember, anything contrary to God's nature is sin. In order for us to live up to God's character and standards and receive His greatest blessings, we must be pure in every area of our lives — including the area of sexual activity. This is emphasized over and over in the Bible:

> But among you there must not be even a hint of
> sexual immorality, or of any kind of impurity, or of
> greed, because these are improper for God's holy
> people. (Ephesians 5:3)

> It is God's will that you should be sanctified: that
> you should avoid sexual immorality; that each of
> you should learn to control his own body in a
> way that is holy and honorable, not in passionate
> lust like the heathen, who do not know God.
> (1 Thessalonians 4:3-5)

The Song of Solomon, the fifth chapter of Proverbs, and many other verses in the Bible make it obvious that God wants sexual relationships to be enjoyable, but they also unmistakably point out that these relationships are only to take place within the boundaries of a marriage. That means that any sexual activity outside marriage is impure. In 1 Corinthians 7:1-9, Paul talks about the sexual obligations of a husband and a wife. He, too, makes it very clear that sex outside marriage is wrong. He even commands anyone who is filled with passion to go ahead and get married before they blow it and sin!

Fornication (a big word for premarital sex) and adultery (sex engaged in by a married person outside his or her own marriage) are both prohibited many times in the Bible. I won't list all the references here, but you can look them up in a concordance if you are interested. Fornication is mentioned thirty-six times and adultery is mentioned forty times in *Strong's Exhaustive Concordance of the Bible*. That's a lot — considering holiness is only mentioned forty-three times!

According to 1 John 4:8, God is not only pure; He is also a God of love. And the characteristics of His love are defined for us in 1 Corinthians 13. Verse 7 tells us that God's love "always protects, always trusts, always hopes, always perseveres." And that's the kind of love we're supposed to have in our relationships.

Many of your friends believe that if you truly love someone, that makes it *all right* to have a sexual relationship outside marriage. But according to God's definition of love, true love actually makes it *all wrong*! True love puts the happiness, health, and spiritual growth of the other person above its own desires. Therefore true love does not engage in any activity that could possibly harm somone or lead another person to sin.

Lust, however, is a different story. Lust looks after its *own* needs and desires. God did not create lust. It showed up in the Garden of Eden when sin entered the world. It is mankind's perversion of the beautiful commitment and emotion that God created for our pleasure. It is the opposite of love.

Love builds others up for their good.	*Lust uses others for personal gain.*
Love gives what it has to others.	*Lust gets what it wants regardless of others.*
Love is patient and understanding.	*Lust is impatient and pushy.*
Love desires to satisfy.	*Lust demands more.*
Love looks at the future.	*Lust only sees right now.*

Don't ever mistake lust for love!

God's rules and regulations for sexual relationships are very clear. Our relationships must be pure (according to God's standards of purity) and loving (according to God's standards of love). To be totally pure and truly loving, sex can only take place within the boundaries of marriage. Based on God's character and His written Word (the Bible), *any* sexual activity outside marriage is wrong.

WHY DID GOD DESIGN THIS STANDARD?

This boundary called "marriage" that God placed around the enjoyment of sexual pleasure exists to protect us and provide for our good. If we step outside of it, what was meant to be magnificent and beautiful can suddenly become horrifying and ugly.

When we watch a television show about lions, it's hard not to be moved by the beauty and strength of such magnificent creatures. But if a lion escaped from the zoo at Busch Gardens in Tampa and walked down our street, we would be filled with terror. Outside the places we have designated for them, untamed creatures impose great threats.

The same thing is true about fireworks. The explosions that fill us with wonder and amazement when they are ignited at the stadium downtown on a starry Fourth of July night can wreak havoc if they are accidentally set off in a factory or storage shed. Their power and potential are frightening.

I guarantee you that the strength of your sexual passions will sometimes frighten you. God loaded you full of them so that when the proper time comes for them to be ignited, they will explode in huge flashes of glory like the best fireworks display you have ever seen! But meanwhile, they must be kept carefully packaged and under control. They must not be exposed to anything that could accidentally set them off. They are wild and wonderful, yet they can become wicked when ignited outside the area God designated for their use.

God designed intercourse to take place only within the limits of a lifetime commitment. That's because no matter how many times or how frequently someone tells you, "I will love you forever" — they won't. Every relationship (whether it involves marriage or not) goes through a "falling out of love" stage at some point. Unless that relationship is tied together by marriage vows and strong family commitments, the "falling out of love stage" usually causes it to end. The "I'll love you forever" feelings and promises that often cause teens to give in to their passions and engage in premarital sex eventually pass, often leaving deep wounds and resulting in permanent scars.

1. Enjoying sex only in the context of marriage protects us from guilt and fear and gives us peace of mind.

Indulging in sexual activity outside marriage almost always leaves those involved with tremendous feelings of guilt. And, as we have mentioned before, guilt is a heavy burden to bear. It robs us of joy and fills us with shame. It makes us less likely to pursue new friendships and more likely to withdraw from old relationships as we try to hide our exploits from those who love us most. It impacts all the other people each partner is related to. It can lead to feelings of low self-esteem, and it can result in heartache and heartbreak.

Sexual activity can also cause tremendous anxiety. The fear of an unplanned pregnancy and the decisions and financial pressures that it would bring can be overwhelming. And the constant threat of acquiring some form of sexually transmitted disease (STD) is very real and very stressful.

There is no method of birth control that is one hundred percent effective — especially in the inexperienced hands of passionate youth. And no contraception has been invented that can stop all STDs. The truth of the matter is that there is no such thing as "safe sex."

A. C. Green, who played basketball from 1985-2001, put it this way: "No man or woman, boy or girl, should put their trust in a piece of rubber. A condom never stopped a person from experiencing a broken heart or a shattered dream no matter how many you put on. For singles — *safe sex is no sex*. Period. That's a one hundred percent guarantee."[1]

Waiting for marriage eliminates all guilt and fear and allows for tremendous freedom and peace of mind. This freedom and peace lead to beautiful expressions of love in the marriage bed.

2. Enjoying sex only in the context of marriage protects us from addiction and keeps us whole.

You know that nicotine and alcohol can lead to addiction and problems in some people's lives. Premarital sex can do the same. Sex can become a crutch that people fall back on when experiencing feelings of insecurity or worthlessness. For a few brief moments they can feel a sense of accomplishment and belonging. Unfortunately, they are just as likely to feel pain and low self-esteem when the accomplishment is evaluated in the light of day and the feelings of belonging vanish as the sun peeks up over the horizon. A vicious cycle of unhealthy behavior can easily begin.

Sex involves much more than two physically naked bodies. It includes emotional, spiritual, and mental nakedness as well. That is why many teenagers find it so difficult to break up with someone with whom they have been intimate.

Just this week our newspaper carried the story of a local boy who was on trial for murdering his ex-girlfriend. It is one of the saddest cases our town has ever experienced. The girlfriend had broken off their relationship, which had just begun to involve sexual activity. But it wasn't just her boyfriend's physical body that she was rejecting and discarding. It was the very essence of who he was — his mind, his will, and his emotions. He couldn't bear to live without her, and he couldn't stand the thought of her living with anyone else. So he took her life.

To refrain from any sexual activity outside marriage is the only way to guarantee that none of these painful behaviors will become a part of your life.

3. Enjoying sex only in the context of marriage protects marriage partners and maintains respect and trust.

When you engage in sexual activities, you give away a part of yourself that you can never take back or give to the person you eventually want to spend the rest of your life loving. You also remove the "trust factor" from a future marriage relationship. You see, if your marriage partner knows you are willing to obey God through the pressures and temptations of this one very challenging standard, it is much easier for him or her to trust you in other areas as well.

Purity and love in sexual relationships lead to maximum pleasure in sexuality. There is never any fear of hidden diseases or emotional damage. If you and your partner each enter your marriage relationship sexually pure, I can guarantee that you will experience incomparable intimacy and pleasure. This is one of the greatest gifts God can give to His children.

WHY IS IT SO HARD TO ACCEPT THIS STANDARD?

Handling sexual relationships is one area of life in which the ways of the world completely contradict the wisdom and standards of God. Unfortunately, through television, movies, magazines, and even sex education courses, you are exposed to the world's views far more frequently and convincingly than you are taught the principles of God. Sex is the punch line for almost every joke, the drawing card for almost every movie, the bottom line of almost every magazine article, and the top concern on the minds of most of your friends.

The entertainment industry makes it not only desirable, but also necessary to have sex in order to be cool. Their philosophy seems to be that in order to make wise choices about sex, you have to experience it. This is ridiculous. Contrary to modern thought, personal experiences and feelings are not the only way to "know" something.

Do you have to use drugs to find out if addiction is right or wrong? Do you have to abuse alcohol to grasp its debilitating effects? Do you have to attempt suicide to learn more about its causes? Do you have to experience rape or genocide to cry out against human atrocities? Absolutely not! Instead of enhancing your decision-making process, experimentation often limits your abilities to make wise choices. This is definitely true in the examples of drug or alcohol abuse. And it would be impossible to make wise choices concerning suicide after one successful attempt. Sex education is no different. You do not need to try something to know all that you need to know about it.

Another very important matter that the media has handled completely incorrectly is the subject of oral sex. You may not know what that is just yet, but you need to know that it is wrong. In God's eyes, oral sex is just what we have named it — sex! Any act that involves stimulation of the genitals or copulation in any manner is an act of sexual impurity unless it takes place between a husband and wife.

The media is totally wrong when it comes to disseminating information about the role of sex in our lives. But so are our schools! Educators insist that because you're going to do it anyway, it's our job to show you how to do it safely. Unfortunately, they are deluding themselves about their role, degrading your intelligence, and deceiving you about your safety.

Some promote the idea that having sex is merely the fulfillment of a natural, animal drive that we have inherited from our evolutionary ancestors. This is completely wrong, not to mention demeaning. We are not merely animals. In His creative order, God placed us only slightly lower than the angels. (Read Psalm 8 if you don't believe me!) We can do more than just react to our instincts. We have been given the ability to choose how and why and when and where we will act. Sex is not merely a natural human function. It is a profound expression of oneness — a unity of body, mind, and spirit. Sex, for us, carries with it a promise of love.

Add to media misinformation and educational inaccuracies the fact that your body is (or soon will be) surging with hormones and your peers are (or soon will be) pressuring you relentlessly to engage in sexual activity, and you find yourself in the middle of a pressure-packed powder keg! But listen to what a seventeen-year-old high school senior who was a virgin told her friends who were pressuring her:

> Look, I don't want any more pressure about me
> becoming sexually involved or jokes about my vir-
> ginity, because each one of you needs to realize
> that whenever I want to I can become like you, but
> you can never again become like me.[2]

God's power in you through the Holy Spirit is more powerful than any other pressures you will ever face. You don't *have* to give in!

In every poll I found while researching this subject, more than 70 percent of the young adults surveyed claimed to have been sexually active during their teenage years (most often it was over 75 percent). This is a very sad statistic given the tremendous blessings God has in store for those who live by His standards. But an even sadder statistic I found is that Christian teenagers' sexual activity is almost as great as that of their nonChristian friends.

Churches and parents have failed. We have not been bold enough to stand up and discredit the foolish philosophies of the world. We have allowed you to accept the values and myths of a God-forsaking culture and to experiment with philosophies that can threaten your lives. You are going to have to take the situation into your own hands and stand up for what you know is right.

HOW CAN YOU LIVE UP TO GOD'S STANDARDS?

St. Francis of Assisi called his body "Brother Ass." (Hang in here with me. I'm not trying to be crude.) He recognized that his body, just like a donkey, was lazy and stubborn. And just like a donkey, it was a follower — not a leader. The rider determined where his body went, and the rider, he explained, was his mind.[3]

On their own, our bodies cannot decide where they will go. Their riders do. Our thought lives and our decisions determine what we will do with our physical bodies. Therefore, it is crucial for us to keep our minds pure. Second Corinthians 10:5 tells us that we must "take captive every thought." We cannot let our imaginations escape to places they should not go. That means that *all* forms of pornography and sexually oriented entertainment must be eliminated from our lives. We cannot expect our bodies to remain clean and pure if our minds are taking them down filthy paths. We cannot expose our thoughts to sex and expect our bodies not to follow.

Girls need to understand something about guys. God designed males to be turned on by sight. For a girl to dress provocatively in order to attract a guy's attention to her body is wrong. Short shorts and low-cut or tight-fitting tops are enticing lures that lead a guy's mind down sinful paths. In 1 Corinthians 10:31-32, God tells us that in *whatever* we do, we must do it all for the glory of God. Then He adds this command, *"Do not cause anyone to stumble."*

And guys, God designed female bodies to respond to physical touch. It is wrong for you to lay a hand on a girl in any way that would stimulate her sexual desires.

The only way to live up to God's standards is to make the decision that you will remain pure until marriage. But exactly how much physical contact can you have with the opposite sex before it becomes sinful?

1. Think through the dating process.

The Bible makes it very clear that any sexual intercourse outside marriage is wrong, but it remains fairly silent about all the acts that lead up to intercourse. Have you ever wondered why that is? I sure have!

Recently I discovered that in the cultures during which most of the Scriptures were written, the Jewish men and women hardly saw each other before they were married. Most marriages were arranged and most brides and grooms had no opportunity for intimacy prior to the ceremony. They were kept apart.

Do you remember the story of Isaac and Rebekah in Genesis 24? The first time Isaac laid eyes on Rebekah, she was riding across his plantation on a camel. A servant had gone to a foreign land in search of the perfect bride. Isaac had never even spoken to her. But as soon as she stepped down off that camel, they were married. There was no time for premarital closeness or familiarity. There was no reason for them to ever question how or where they should or should not touch.

Marriage was handled in very much the same way during New Testament times. Because no chance for intimacy existed prior to marriage, there was no need for mandates regarding premarital pressures. Petting was not much of an option and therefore not much of a problem. That's why Peter and Paul and other writers did not discuss it in any detail.

But the dating rituals of our culture are entirely different. We find ourselves having to answer the question "How far is too far?" It is a decision that you need to make *before* you find yourself hormone-deep in a situation where you cannot think or reason clearly. It is a line you must draw for yourself. It is a line that you must not allow anyone or anything to force you to cross.

Let me describe for you the steps that most physical relationships pass through as they head toward sexual intercourse.

A close relationship most often begins with holding hands. It is sometimes a magical, tingling moment when those two hands meet and grasp each other in more than a casual encounter.

This step is usually followed by physical horseplay — like rough-housing in the swimming pool or wrestling for something that belongs to you that the other person has grabbed.

This can lead to embracing and cuddling and a physical relationship that includes short kisses and caressing — mostly of faces and necks. There is usually more eye contact than physical contact at this stage.

If a line is not drawn and agreed upon, the relationship can quickly advance to long, steamy, passionate kissing with a lot of clothed bodily contact.

In the next step, the hands sneak beneath the clothing, and touching of the breasts and genitals begins.

The only stage left is sexual intercourse.

Based on God's demands for total purity and true love, we know that anything that will stimulate our partner to desire to engage in sexual behavior is wrong. That makes touching a partner's breasts or genitals in any way totally out of the picture if you want to abide by

God's standards and enjoy His blessings. Any heavy petting, even on top of the clothing, is also wrong because of the feelings it arouses.

But everything between holding hands and long, hot, engaging kisses (such as French kisses) falls into a fuzzy area. That's because something that is sexually arousing for one person might not be for another. What is a mild expression of affection for one person might be a complete "turn on" for another. You and your dating partner have to decide where you will draw the line that separates "pure" dating actions from "sinful" dating actions.

In a letter to his son, Sean, Josh McDowell describes acceptable physical contact this way: "You can happily share all those physical contacts which don't raise desires in either you or your girlfriend which cannot righteously be fulfilled."[4] Notice the word *righteously*. No matter how wonderful or beautiful the feeling may be, the action is not righteous if it causes either of you to desire to move on to something that you know God would not approve.

2. Establish your own boundaries.

There are several decisions that you need to make before you begin to date someone seriously. If you do this now, you will not be forced to make extremely important, life-altering choices in the heat of passion. I have listed a few that I think are absolutely mandatory if you truly desire to obey God's standards of love and purity. You need to add your own to the list. I encourage you to write them down and sign your name. Then place them in the back of your Bible or in the glove compartment of your car — as soon as you have one — so that you will constantly be aware of them.

- I will never go into a bedroom or crawl into the back seat of a car with my date.
- I will never explore my date's body or allow my date to explore mine.

- I will not look at books or magazines or TV shows or movies or listen to music that will cause me to desire sexual contact.
- I will not date a person who has a reputation based on sensuality or sexuality.

When you start to date someone seriously, it would be very wise to go over your list together and verbally commit to each other that you will abide by these standards — and any others that your dating partner wishes to add. Then refer to them often.

3. Make tangible commitments.

I want to emphasize the importance of having tangible, concrete symbols that are constant reminders of the commitments you have made to yourself and to God. When each of you boys turned sixteen we presented you with a key — a fourteen-carat-gold key — on a gold chain to be worn around your neck. We explained to you that it is a gift that you are to present to your wife on your wedding night, symbolizing the purity you will maintain as you wait to share your body with her. It is a pledge that your body has never been, nor ever will be, given away to anyone else. It is to be your wife's and hers alone.

The key also symbolizes the fact that we, as your parents, are fully aware of the temptations and pressures you face every day in our society. It concretely visualizes the promise that we will continually pray for you and that you must fully obey God's standards if you want to enjoy His blessings and rewards. It is a tangible sign of our expectations — not just our hopes!

If no one else will provide these symbols for you, you must provide them for yourself! You must grasp onto the commitments you have made in concrete, tangible ways or they may be forgotten when they are most needed.

There is just one more thing I want to say. If anyone reading this has already overstepped God's boundaries and has engaged in sexual activity outside marriage, I want to remind you that it is never too late to start doing what is right. God promises both forgiveness and restoration. Yes, you will experience some of the consequences we have mentioned, but you will also experience His healing and His help if you ask Him for them. If you are struggling right now because you have already blown it, but you want to start living your life according to God's standards and experience His forgiveness and joy, go ahead and turn to Dilemma #10 on page 143. I'll meet you there, and we'll talk more about God's unbelievable love.

SUMMARY

Sex outside marriage is sin. God placed sexual activity within the boundary of marriage for our protection and for our pleasure. Only by abiding by His standards, which include total purity and true love, and by obeying His commands in the Bible to keep the marriage bed pure (see Hebrews 13:4) can we experience the fullness of this wonderful, beautiful gift.

You are constantly exposed to extreme pressure and misinformation from the entertainment industry, the educational system, and your peers. It is far too easy in this culture to give in to sexual passions. But you must not! You must make decisions ahead of time that will guard your thoughts and protect your body. You must grab onto concrete, tangible symbols that will remind you daily of the commitments you have made. Don't invalidate the blessings of one of the most beautiful gifts God wants to give you by opening it before you are supposed to.

DILEMMA #6

ISN'T HOMOSEXUALITY A VALID *Lifestyle Alternative?*

DAD AND I WERE IN ESTES PARK, COLORADO, LAST SUMMER FOR A CONFERence. The scenery, the weather, the people — *everything* was just wonderful. (July in Colorado is certainly a whole lot more fun than July in Florida!) One afternoon, we were given extra free time, so we decided to take a sightseeing trip with some friends. We drove into Rocky Mountain National Park and stopped near a lake. We walked around the water for a while, enjoying the peaceful scenery, then we decided to take a trail deep into the forest that led to another lake about two miles away — at least that's what the sign said.

We followed the path as closely as we could, but sometimes we had to take little detours to get around toppled trees or recently fallen boulders. We always managed to scramble our way back to what we thought was the trail. It turned out to be quite a strenuous trek, much more steep and difficult than we had anticipated.

After hiking for what seemed like two hours, we finally broke into a clearing. We were shocked to find that we were on the edge of a cliff overlooking a huge valley. All we could see for miles were the tops of trees leading to a spectacular vista of mountains covered with snow. We were obviously not anywhere near the lake we were looking for. As a matter of fact, we were completely lost. We had traveled in a totally different direction than we meant to — even though every turn we had taken seemed entirely right!

We sat at the edge of the cliff for a few minutes enjoying the scenery and snapping a few pictures. Then we had to make a decision. Should we continue to follow the trail up the mountain, hoping it would lead us somewhere even more unexpected and exciting, or should we turn around and try to find our way back before dark? It was a tough decision. The walk along that cliff was obviously a little treacherous, but it sure did seem inviting. However, wisdom (prompted by age!) prevailed, and we decided to head down before the sun set.

Eventually we came to a small road. We followed it until we found some people who gave us directions back to the original lake where we had parked our car. We were a little late for dinner that evening, but we made it safely home before dark.

Right now you might be wondering, *What on earth does that story have to do with homosexuality?* Well, I'm about to tell you.

Just as we never made an active decision to wind up on the edge of that mountain cliff in the middle of Rocky Mountain National Park, I don't believe that most gay men or lesbian women made conscious decisions to become homosexuals. We were headed toward a lake, but toppled trees and fallen boulders along the park trail got in our way and caused us to change directions without even realizing it. I believe that the same thing happens with people who practice homosexuality. I think various deterrents and distractions along the paths of their lives cause them to wind up in emotional places where they never planned to go.

It is very important before we go any further to distinguish between homosexual feelings and homosexual behavior. *Homosexual feelings* are the desires that a person has for someone of the same sex to provide emotional intimacy, acceptance, and affection. *Homosexual behavior* is choosing to act on those feelings and establishing a sexual relationship with a person of the same sex.

People do not necessarily choose their feelings, but they do choose how they will react to them. Let me say that again so I'm sure that you've got it. *A person does not necessarily choose the feelings that he or she is going to have, but each person is responsible for what to do with those feelings when they arrive.*

Some of the deterrents and distractions that cause people to veer off the "straight" path and develop feelings of homosexuality have to do with certain physical or emotional traumas that they faced as young children. Sexual abuse during childhood or adolescence is often a strong factor in determining an adult sexual orientation. Because of the special attention, and sometimes even gifts, that a boy might receive from an abusing male, he will sometimes feel that the only place he can find love and acceptance is with another male — especially if he experiences rejection from a female sometime during his adolescent years. A girl who is abused by a male, on the other hand, may develop such hatred and bitterness for males that she eventually turns to females for all her support. (The reverse is true if it is a woman who is the abuser, although such cases don't seem to be as common.)

Homosexual feelings can develop in a child who has experienced cruel teasing and rejection by his or her peers. The insecure thoughts of being "different" or unwanted are sometimes interpreted later as early feelings of homosexuality. Peers who decide to experiment with each other's sexuality can also introduce each other to homosexual feelings. And I was surprised to find that hostile relationships with older brothers (for a male) and sisters (for a female) can lead to feelings of homosexuality, as the child struggles to be as different as possible from the mean older sibling.

Also, if children do not have parents or adults in their lives who effectively model masculinity or femininity for them, they are more likely to develop homosexual tendencies than children who are able to observe traditional maleness and femaleness in their daily lives.[1]

Sometimes the feelings associated with a normal adolescent stage of deep admiration for a role model of the same sex are later misinterpreted. A teenager or adult is led to believe that earlier feelings of respect and esteem were really the first signs of a gay orientation.

As you can see, homosexual feelings are often the result of emotional traumas that were never dealt with when they occurred during childhood or adolescence. They can develop out of unmet needs for love and support. Or they can come from emotional feelings that are misinterpreted later in life.

Instead of looking for God's way to fulfill their needs and fix their hurt feelings and damaged emotions, people often come up with their own ways. Homosexual behavior is the result of an inner drive to fix things that are wrong. It is a way of trying to meet those needs and resolve those injured feelings and emotions. Unfortunately, it can often lead to much more pain and trauma. Let's look at what God says about homosexuality.

WHAT IS GOD'S STANDARD REGARDING HOMOSEXUALITY?

As we mentioned in the last chapter, one of God's characteristics is that He is completely pure. Therefore, if we are going to live according to His standards, we must choose to live pure lives, and that includes our sexual relationships. I hope that I was able to make it very clear in the last chapter that according to God's standards, any sexual relationship outside marriage is sin. We talked about how this includes fornication (sex before marriage) and adultery (sex outside marriage). And now we will discuss how it also includes homosexuality.

In Genesis 1–2, God gives us His blueprint for human sexuality, His design for where and why sex is supposed to take place and who is supposed to be involved. When God first created Adam, He created him without a partner. Each of the other animals was part of a matching set. Adam even got to name them as God brought *all* the animals before him in pairs. (My guess is that he must have been pretty tired by the time he got around to naming the aardvarks!) During the process, I'm sure it became apparent to Adam that he was missing something. He was the only creature that was all alone, the only one who didn't have a female to stand by his side. Obviously, he realized that some of his needs were not being met.

I don't think God goofed here and later realized that He needed to add Eve to help Adam out. I think God wanted Adam to realize that he was incomplete without Eve. He wanted Adam to understand that he was missing something and that the hole in his life could only be filled by the precious gift God was about to create — a woman. He was to find his emotional, social, and sexual fulfillment by uniting his life with hers.

When God presented Adam with Eve, Adam was ecstatic. He knew that his search for companionship was over, that the empty spaces in his life had been filled. God's editorial comment recorded for us in Genesis 2:24 says, "For this reason a man will leave his father and mother and be united to his wife, and they will become one flesh."

God's original blueprint for sexual relationships required that they take place between a man and a woman within the boundaries of a lifetime commitment of love — called marriage. And sex within that marriage is designed to provide pleasure and create new life. Yes, one of the purposes for sex is to have children. This can only take place in a heterosexual relationship.

Jesus reiterates and reinforces this blueprint in the New Testament. When questioned about marriage in Matthew 19:1-12 and Mark 10:1-12, He could have responded with a different design based on His God-given authority. He did that many times — like when He taught that we should turn the other cheek rather than insist on getting even (see Matthew 5:38-39). But this time He chose to reaffirm God's original plan for marriage — the plan of heterosexual love within a lifetime commitment.

This blueprint alone, established in the Old Testament and reiterated in the New, is enough for us to understand what brings God pleasure in a marriage. It provides plenty of information to keep us from accepting same-sex partnerships as a Christian option. But God states His views on homosexuality even more clearly than this.

Do you remember the time I got very angry with the four of you for swimming in the pond behind our old house after I had specifically told you not to? We were planning to go to the mall, but I had a few things to do before we could leave. You begged me to let you go outside and play until I was ready. I was hesitant, but I decided it was okay as long as you didn't get wet and dirty. I remember hollering out the door, "Whatever you do, don't go swimming."

When I called you inside, you were all soaking wet. I was furious.

"We weren't swimming!" you insisted. "We were just wading — and maybe we were floating a little. But we never moved our arms and legs and actually went *swimming*!"

Technically, you might have been right. But according to my standards you were wrong, because the intent of my warning was clear and obvious. However, from then on I made my intentions very clear. If I did not want you to get wet I plainly stated that you were not allowed to get even a single drop of water anywhere on your clothing or your body!

God knows how devious we can be and how easy it is for us to try to rationalize our way around His standards and wind up doing things that are not pleasing to Him. So He states His standard for sexual purity concerning homosexuality even more obviously for us than He did in Genesis 1–2. In Leviticus 18:22 and 20:13 He says, "Do not lie with a man as one lies with a woman; that is detestable" and "If a man lies with a man as one lies with a woman, both of them have done what is detestable. They must be put to death." I think that's pretty clear!

But some people argue that the same collection of laws in Leviticus that condemns homosexuality also says it is wrong to plant two kinds of seeds in one field or to eat pork. They point out that people do both of these things all the time, yet nobody seems to get all bent out of shape. "How can you insist that people have to follow one law and not all the others?" they want to know.

They make a good point. But what they fail to understand is that three different kinds of laws were given in the Old Testament. There were *civil laws* that defined specifically how the Israelites were to live as a nation. There were also *ceremonial laws* that dealt mostly with the regulations for how they were to sacrifice and worship God in the tabernacle. And there were *moral laws* that commanded them how to live in a relationship with a sovereign God and with each other.

Following Christ's death on the cross and His resurrection, the civil laws became unnecessary. There was no longer a separate nation (the Jews) through whom everyone had to come if they wanted to know God. Instead of a *national* relationship with God governed by civil laws, Christ opened the way for individuals to have a *personal* relationship with God.

There was also no longer a need for a tabernacle or a temple or priests to help with worship, because each person could approach God on his or her own. So all the sacrifices and ceremonies regulated by the ceremonial laws stopped having any significance as well. The *principles* of how to live well in a society and how to worship a holy God that were found in the civil and ceremonial laws of the Old Testament are still valid, but the specific laws are no longer mandatory for us today.

The third kind of laws given in the Old Testament — the *moral laws* — described exactly how God wanted His people to live in a relationship with Him and with each other. They are found in the Ten Commandments and expanded in other passages. All of them, except the law to keep the Sabbath as a holy day, were reiterated and expanded upon in the New Testament, particularly by Christ in the Sermon on the Mount. And, although the punishments were changed with Christ's coming, all of them (except the law regarding the Sabbath) are still binding for us.

The passages in Leviticus that deal with homosexuality are part of God's *moral law* concerning adultery. They still apply to us. All sexual relationships that did not take place between a man and a woman within the boundaries of a marriage were improper and impure during Old Testament times, and they still are wrong today. This includes homosexuality.

A startling story of sexual perversion occurs in Genesis 18–19. It tells of an attempted gang rape of two angels who came as men to visit Lot in the city of Sodom. God harshly judged and punished the men involved in the homosexual activity. They were struck blind, and the next day the city was destroyed with fire and brimstone.

Homosexuality is very clearly forbidden in the New Testament as well. In Romans 1:24-32, God describes sexual relationships with a person of the same sex as "indecent," a "perversion," and "depraved." And in 1 Corinthians 6:9-11 He lists "homosexual offenders" among the "wicked (who) will not inherit the kingdom of God."

God is the Creator and Boss of the universe. He is the One who defines the dimensions of Right and Wrong, and He does so in absolute terms. Based on His character and purity and according to the standards He details for us in the Bible, it is very clear that God detests acts of homosexuality. They are contrary to His character and in direct opposition to His laws.

WHY DID GOD DESIGN THIS STANDARD?

As we have said, God designed for us to find sexual fulfillment in the context of a lifetime commitment to a partner of the opposite sex. And just as a river that rushes over its banks can cause great damage and destruction, sexual activity that ignores the boundaries God has established for it can lead to many problems and much pain in the lives of those who practice it. Homosexual behavior definitely does not flow within the boundaries God has established for sexual behavior.

1. Sex in the context of God's design protects us from shame, anger, and loneliness and provides great joy.

Do you remember the story of Cain and Abel in the Bible? Cain was the oldest son of Adam and Eve, and Abel was his younger brother. Cain loved to work in the fields, planting and digging and weeding and harvesting. Abel, on the other hand, spent most of his time working with the animals.

When it came time for them to make a sacrifice to God, Cain brought an offering of fresh fruits and vegetables from his fields, and Abel brought one of the animals from his flocks. Genesis 4:4-5 tells us that "The Lord looked with favor on Abel and his offering, but on Cain and his offering he did not look with favor."

The problem wasn't that God didn't like Cain as much as He liked Abel. The problem was that Cain's sacrifice was not within the boundaries that God had established. Beginning with the very first sin (when Adam and Eve deliberately ate fruit from the tree that God had told them not to eat from), God made it clear that a blood sacrifice was necessary for forgiveness. To illustrate this, God Himself sacrificed an animal to make the clothing that covered the nakedness and shame Adam and Eve experienced following their sin.

Cain knew God's requirement, yet he chose to disregard God's standards for sacrifice. When God rejected his garden sacrifice, instead of admitting he was wrong and offering an animal sacrifice, Cain grew bitter and angry. You know the rest of the story. Cain ended up killing his own brother. As a consequence, Cain was alienated from his family and forced to wander the rest of his life. I share this story because it illustrates the shame, bitterness, and loneliness that can accompany *any* sin when a person does not seek forgiveness.

These three feelings are often associated with the practice of homosexuality. Shame can linger from the past experiences that have not been dealt with and that have led to homosexuality. It can also accompany the knowledge that practicing homosexuality is breaking God's laws. Or it can arise from feeling the need to hide one's orientation and lifestyle from friends and other family members who would not approve.

Feeling misunderstood and mistreated can lead to bitterness and anger in the heart of a practicing homosexual. Feelings of rejection can lead to extreme loneliness and despair as a gay (a somewhat ironic name) or lesbian person finds himself or herself isolated from past friendships and/or family relationships. This is one reason why studies of homosexual men find that they are six times more likely to commit suicide than straight men and four times more likely to be alcoholics.[2]

Sex was not meant to create such turmoil. God created sex as a beautiful source of joy and fulfillment. And when practiced within the boundaries He established, it provides just that! Within the context of a loving heterosexual marriage, sex can bring enjoyment and pleasure that cannot be duplicated anywhere else.

2. Sex in the context of God's design protects us from illness and stress.

In the last chapter we talked about the stress that often accompanies sexual relationships outside marriage. One cause of such stress is the fear of the many horrible sexually transmitted illnesses. These fears are multiplied in the case of homosexuality, because the same illnesses are a threat to the homosexual population, along with a much higher risk of contracting HIV. The incidence of AIDS is far greater among practicing homosexuals than it is among the "straight" population.

Directly opposed to this is the freedom and peace of mind that accompany sex practiced within the boundaries of a loving heterosexual marriage. Fear and anxiety are removed, replaced instead with a relaxed atmosphere of trust and tranquility.

3. Sex in the context of God's design protects the human race and provides the blessing of new life.

When God created Eve in order to complete and complement Adam, He included a wonderful gift called "sex" as part of their union. One of the greatest blessings and main functions of their sexual activity was the creation of new life. As a matter of fact, God commanded them to fill the whole earth with kids (see Genesis 1:28).

God designed this by-product of sex not only as the means to propagate the human species, but as a way to bring joy and blessing into the life of married couples. Psalm 127:3 describes children as "a reward" from God. They are a vital and wonderful part of God's design for marriage.

Obviously, homosexual relationships do not allow for this process known as procreation. They negate the potential for creating new life, and thus deny God's design and His blessing.

WHY IS IT SO HARD TO ACCEPT THIS STANDARD?

Many people in our society have chosen to view homosexuality as an acceptable, alternative lifestyle. And they want everyone else to agree with them! They present several arguments that seem reasonable unless looked at carefully.

Advocates of homosexuality describe it as a "preference." They try to make it a decision as harmless as, *"Would you prefer to spend the evening at a baseball game or would you rather attend a rock concert?"* when it is actually a choice that involves acceptance or rejection of God's sovereignty and His standards. It is a choice that carries with it grave consequences.

Homosexual activists also argue that a gay lifestyle arises out of "natural" feelings and instincts, therefore it cannot be wrong. However, just because something is "natural" does not necessarily make it right. The "natural" reaction for a young child whose pajamas catch on fire is to run as fast as he or she can to try to escape from the flames. But the right thing to do, as you have been taught many times, is to "stop, drop, and roll." The "natural" reaction to a flaming pair of pajamas is actually the worst thing that could take place. Natural instincts are often very harmful.

Plus, as I have already pointed out, the "natural" feelings of homosexuality are often caused by past physical or emotional traumas that have rerouted proper feelings and sent them in the wrong direction.

When an entire pod of pilot whales beaches itself off the coast of New England, as they sometimes do, it is a natural instinct that leads them into such disaster. No one knows for sure why the whales do this, but it is believed that this destructive instinct is triggered by some kind of trauma. It may be disease or navigational error or both. And in the close-knit society of pilot whales, if one whale heads in the wrong direction, the others almost always do so as well. "Natural" feelings can be very misguiding.

Many scientists believe that homosexuality is the result of inherited genes, and this may be the case. Many experiments have been done to try to document this, but, so far, every time there appears to be empirical evidence, further study causes it to evaporate.

As a matter of fact, some scientific studies seem to indicate the opposite. If homosexuality were inherited, all identical twins would either have the gene or not have it — because their genes are exact duplicates. But there are thousands of identical twins in which one is gay and the other is straight.[3]

What's more, inherited characteristics that are not passed on are eliminated from a gene pool. Fewer lesbian women and gay men have children than heterosexual couples. It is true that some choose to suppress their homosexual feelings, and therefore have children with a heterosexual mate. In such cases, if there were such a gene, it would be passed on in a limited amount. But logically, doesn't it seem that there should be a steady decrease in the number of people with homosexual tendencies? That doesn't appear to be happening.

Even if one day it is proven that homosexuality is genetically determined, that does not make homosexual behavior acceptable in God's sight. God has made it very clear that it is a misuse of His gift of sexuality, and it is destructive to those He loves. When doctors learn that a person is genetically predisposed to cancer or heart disease, they help that person adjust his or her lifestyle as much as possible to avoid the consequences of that biological predisposition. If a person has a genetic tendency toward alcoholism, it doesn't excuse him or her to live a life of drunkenness. Both nonChristian and Christian sources confirm that many homosexuals are able to change their orientation. Many have made an active decision to leave behind a lifestyle of homosexuality and become "straight."

Because of sin, we live in a fallen, imperfect world. Genetic brokenness is one of the consequences, but it never excuses us from living according to God's standards. God is a just God. He would not condemn anything as an abominable sin if we could not choose to abstain from it (see 1 Corinthians 10:13).

Although this has become a very volatile subject in our society, the critical issue isn't what *I* think of homosexuality, or what *you* think of it, or what someone marching in a parade to get his or her viewpoint across thinks. The issue is: What does *God* think based on what He has conveyed to us in the Bible?

HOW CAN YOU LIVE UP TO GOD'S STANDARD?

Our society says that homosexuality is a result of natural feelings. God says that it is a result of imperfect circumstances. Our society claims that it is an involuntary genetic condition. God says that it is a voluntary choice. Our society insists that it is a harmless option. God says that it is sin with grave consequences. The decision that has to be made is whether or not you will agree with what society promotes or believe and live according to God's standards.

Busch Gardens in Tampa, Florida, has a new adventure ride called Rhino Rally. It is an off-road safari and river adventure through the simulated wilds of Africa. Special Land Rover vehicles take people across rugged open terrain inhabited by elephants, white rhinos, alligators, cape buffalo, and other assorted untamed creatures. Although the potential for danger is great, travelers are promised they will be safe as long as they stay inside the vehicle. As if all that isn't exciting enough, the ride ends after the Land Rover is trapped on a broken slab of bridge that is ripped off during a flash flood and sent hurtling down a river under a cascading waterfall. This all takes place within eight minutes! And though the events of the journey might be contrived, the wild animals and the raging water are very real.

This is a great picture of what is taking place in our world. God's standards are like the safari Land Rovers. As long as we choose to live within the boundaries of those standards, we are guaranteed God's protection and provision. However, if we step outside them, we are stepping into areas of danger and potential pain.

When God calls something detestable, as He does homosexuality in Leviticus 18:22, I have to believe that it will not make Him very happy if I choose to take part in it. The "preference" isn't quite as tame as, "Would you prefer spending the evening at a baseball game or would you rather attend a rock concert?" It's more like, "Would you prefer spending the evening at a baseball game or would you rather be thrown into a pit seething with hundreds of poisonous snakes?" It's not a very difficult decision when put that way. (But I do believe I'd rather be placed in a pit of poisonous snakes than have to face an angry God! Did you read what

He did to the city of Sodom in Genesis 19?) To choose to practice homosexuality is to choose to disobey God.

The decision to abide by God's standards of right and wrong does not allow us the option to act in unloving and disrespectful ways to those who choose not to. Just like any other person who does not know Christ, homosexuals need to be introduced to His love and forgiveness. Remember, Jesus was more compassionate to the woman caught in the very act of adultery — a capital offense during New Testament times — than He was to the hypocritical Pharisees who went to church all the time (see John 8:1-11). And Jesus is our model for how we are to respond to someone who has chosen to sin.

The choice to practice homosexuality is not an irreversible decision. We looked at some verses in 1 Corinthians 6 where Paul lists "homosexual offenders" among the "wicked (who) will not inherit the kingdom of God." But we must not forget to read verse 11. It says, "And that is what some of you were. But you were washed, you were sanctified, you were justified in the name of the Lord Jesus Christ and by the Spirit of our God." Lives and lifestyles can be changed by Christ's love and forgiveness and the power of the Holy Spirit.

We know that all things are possible with God (see Matthew 19:26), and that there is nothing too hard for Him (see Jeremiah 32:17). Psalm 103:3 tells us that He "forgives all (our) sins and heals all (our) diseases." It is never too late to seek His love and forgiveness. It is possible for people who have participated in a homosexual lifestyle to receive inner healing for their past problems and pain and develop a secure gender identity in the role God intended for them to fill. We know several people who have.

SUMMARY

Although homosexual feelings may have been triggered in a person's life by hurt feelings and damaged emotions, acting on those feelings is wrong. God's design is for *all* sexual relationships to take place between a man and a woman within the boundaries of a lifetime commitment of love — called marriage. According to God's standards for sexual purity, *any* sexual activity outside this boundary is sin.

The practice of homosexuality is contrary to God's standards. God blatantly declares that homosexuality is detestable and destructive. It can lead to shame, anger, loneliness, and disease. And it negates one of God's greatest blessings — the gift of reproduction.

Our society teaches that homosexuality is a harmless option. God says that it is *sin* with grave consequences. Our society says that it is a result of natural feelings. God says that it is a result of imperfect circumstances. Our society says that it is an involuntary genetic condition. God says that it is voluntary choice. The decision that must be made is whether or not we will agree with what society says or believe and live according to God's standards. Only then can we enjoy the blessings He promises to those who love and obey Him. God's love and healing are available to those who have disregarded His standards if they desire it and seek His forgiveness.

DILEMMA #7

WHAT'S THE BIG DEAL ABOUT ABORTION? ISN'T IT A WOMAN'S *Right to Decide What to Do with Her Own Body?*

ONCE UPON A TIME THERE WAS AN EGG. IT WAS JUST AN ORDINARY EGG. But one day it met a sperm that it couldn't resist. The two became one, and miraculous things began to take place. The union of that egg and sperm formed a single cell called a zygote, which contained an amazing forty-six chromosomes that were uniquely its own. *Every* piece of equipment and *all* the instructions it needed to grow and develop into a huge, intricate, unique, and wonderfully complex creature were wrapped up inside that one, tiny package. And, guess what — the creature it became is *you*!

Fourteen days following the union of that egg and sperm (an event known as conception), you became an embryo. At just eighteen days your tiny heart began to beat. By the end of the fourth week you were about the size of a pea, but you were already developing kidneys, a liver, and a digestive tract. Six weeks into the process your brain began to function and transmit waves. At seven weeks you were already one inch long and your vital organs were kicking into gear. You had a face with eyes and a nose. You had a mouth with lips, a tongue, and teeth buds in your gums. Your hands were formed. You had a thumb and your very own set of fingerprints. During the ninth and tenth weeks of gestation, your nerve and muscle connections developed enough that you could feel pain. By the time three months had passed, all of your body systems were present and functioning. You had even begun to grow hair.

From the moment of conception, that one, tiny little cell never stopped working and growing and dividing and multiplying. Now, look at it! It is more than a trillion cells, well on its way to being over six feet tall.

However, during the first nine months of your development, you were so fragile that you never could have survived on your own. That's why God placed you in a sheltered environment, a home where you would be guarded and protected and nurtured and loved until you were strong enough to make it on your own in the world. He placed you in the womb of your mother. (That's me!)

Yet according to the laws of our country and state, at just about any point during that time of protective custody, I had the right to say, "No! I don't want him. Take him out of me and destroy him." With one quick whim of my will I could have done away with the intricate, unique, and wonderfully complex *you* that was growing and developing inside of me.

It's hard to imagine life without you! I wonder what God would have thought had I exercised the right that society so freely offers. Let's look at what the Bible says.

WHAT IS GOD'S STANDARD REGARDING ABORTION?

In Psalm 139, as David is praising God, he says, "For you created my inmost being (every single thing inside me); you knit me together in my mother's womb. I praise you because I am fearfully and wonderfully made; your works are wonderful, I know that full well" (verses 13-14).

According to this psalm, an unborn child is not just another growing embryo or fetus. It is the creative handiwork of God. He is actively and intricately involved in forming every detail of each person long before he or she is ever born.

Isaiah explains God's role in our creation by saying, "This is what the Lord says — he who made you, who formed you in the womb" (Isaiah 44:2). And in Jeremiah 1:5, God is speaking to the prophet Jeremiah when He says, "Before I formed you in the womb I knew you, before you were born I set you apart; I appointed you as a prophet to the nations."

When God looks at a fetus (the developing child within the mother), He doesn't see a lump of tissue with some bones holding it together and a few budding organs scattered around. He sees an entire human being and all its potential. He knows everything about it. He knows the name it will be given, its future accomplishments, and the difficulties it will face. He knows every victory and every failure. God sees an individual person with a unique identity and a complete destiny.

All through the Old and New Testaments, the same words used to describe a child after its birth are used when referring to a child still in the womb. God never makes any distinction between born and unborn life. Both are equally valuable to Him.

In Genesis 25:21, the Bible tells us that Rebekah, Isaac's wife, became pregnant with twins. Verse 22 says, "The *babies* jostled each other within her" (emphasis added). In Job 3:16, a stillborn baby is referred to as "an *infant* who never saw the light of day" (emphasis added).

In Luke 1:41, when Elizabeth, who was pregnant with John the Baptist, heard Mary's greeting at the door of her house, the Bible says that "the *baby* leaped in her womb" (emphasis added). In this same passage, Elizabeth, realizing that Mary is also pregnant addressed her as "the *mother* of my Lord" (verse 43, emphasis added). She not only acknowledges that the fetus is a very distinct (and distinguished) person, she also addresses the lady carrying that life as its mother. A woman does not become a mother at the birth of her child. She becomes a mother when that life is conceived within her. We obviously do not grasp the tremendous physical, emotional, and spiritual significance attached to motherhood when we allow an abortion to take place.

God makes it very clear that He does not want any harm to come to an unborn child. In Exodus 21:22-25, He issues the following commandment: "If men who are fighting hit a pregnant woman and she gives birth prematurely but there is no serious injury, the offender must be fined whatever the woman's husband demands and the court allows. But if there is serious injury you are to take life for life, eye for eye."

These verses describe a scene where two men are fighting and a pregnant lady intervenes. In the first situation, she is injured to the point of going into labor, but both she and the baby survive. A financial fine is necessary, but there is no physical penalty given. The word that is translated "gives birth prematurely" in this passage is the Hebrew word *yatsa*. It literally means "so that her children go out." It is *not* the word *shakol*, which is used in other places in the Bible (like Hosea 9:14) and means miscarriage, although this is what some people want you to believe it means here. The verse refers to the premature birth of a *living* child.

In the second situation, however, the baby is seriously injured or dies. Even though the injury or abortion is accidental, God demands punishment — capital punishment if the baby dies. Obviously, in God's eyes the life of the child in the womb has great value. It is equal to the lives of the grown men who are fighting.

I can't help but wonder, if God demands such a severe penalty for the *accidental* death of an unborn child under the laws He gave to Moses, how much more severely must He judge an abortion performed on *purpose!*

Although abortion is a legal right granted to us under the laws of our country, God does not grant us that same moral right. It is the destruction of what He very clearly views as "life," and God's standard is the preservation of that life.

Several years ago the queen of England presented our town, Lakeland, Florida, with some rare and costly black swans. It was a wonderful gift, and we are very proud of the many beautiful, black swans that now make their home near Lake Morton. But I will never forget the hubbub that took place not long ago when some vandals decided to destroy a few of the black swans' eggs. "How could anyone be so callous and cold?" people wanted to know. "How could they live with themselves after destroying those eggs?" There was a tremendous public outrage at the senseless, juvenile act — and there should have been!

Yet that same day probably a dozen abortions took place in one clinic in our town — and no one said a word.

It baffles me that so many people can fail to see the life hidden in the womb of its mother as having the same value as some black swans' eggs. It bewilders me that they fail to see an unborn child in the same way that God does.

WHY DID GOD DESIGN THIS STANDARD?

If everyone in our society was willing to abide by God's standard of sexual purity (which we talked about in Dilemma #5), the need for abortion would almost disappear. That's because the majority of abortions are performed either to eliminate the inconvenience or destroy the evidence of an out-of-wedlock pregnancy. If all sexual relationships took place within the boundaries of marriage, there would be no teenage pregnancies to worry about or any babies conceived as a result of adulterous affairs.

Conception was designed to create a "family." As we stated in Dilemma #6, God planned children as the by-product of sex not only to propagate the human species but to bring joy and blessing into the lives of married couples. Children are a gift from God (see Psalm 127:3). They are a vital and wonderful part of God's design for marriage, and they are very valuable to Him. He does not give them away meaninglessly.

I was watching an antique show on television the other day. I doubt that any of you happened to see it, as it had nothing at all to do with sports, but the host was asking a man how he happened to become the owner of a fancy blue glass vase. The man replied that he had bought it at a garage sale for about four dollars. The previous owner had been given the vase as a gift by a relative, but evidently he didn't like it very much. (I have to admit, I thought it was kind of gaudy myself.) So he sold it at his wife's garage sale. According to the expert antique dealer, the man who had bought it was now the proud owner of an extremely valuable antique vase worth several thousand dollars.

Obviously, the man who had been given the vase as a gift never grasped its true value. It became a nuisance to him, so he decided to get rid of it. Fortunately, someone came along who understood its value and was willing to pay the paltry price to own it. I can only imagine how upset the man would be if he ever found out how valuable the vase he used to own really is.

You know, that's what happens to many women when they choose to have an abortion. They fail to grasp the idea that the life forming within them is a gift from God. Instead, they view it as an inconvenience, a nuisance, or maybe even a punishment. They decide that their lives would be better off without it, and they dispose of it. But a terminated pregnancy often leaves behind a gnawing emptiness. God intended for us to preserve the pregnancies He allows us to have and to enjoy the precious children He has chosen to create.

1. Preserving a pregnancy protects God's handiwork and produces a valuable life.

Abortion not only terminates a pregnancy, it terminates God's plan. We have looked at several verses that tell us how intricately God is involved in forming the features and facts of the life developing in the womb. He is involved in the process from the moment of conception. Whether we choose to call it life at that point or not, it is His creation, and it has tremendous value in His eyes. To destroy it would be to destroy His purpose and plan.

I can't remember all the details of the picture or the exact words in the caption, but several years ago a newspaper cartoon captured a lot of attention. It showed a person kneeling in prayer. He was pleading with God to please send someone smart to earth real soon who would discover the cure for cancer.

"I did. I sent him several years ago," God responded, "but he was aborted!"

Sure makes you ponder for a while, doesn't it! Abortion not only tragically ends the life of a child, it messes with the future of our families and our society.

2. Preserving a pregnancy protects and promotes the well-being of the baby, the mother, and the father.

Many studies show that abortions greatly impact the emotional state of the mothers involved. Often these emotional reactions don't occur right away, but are triggered by some event (like the birth of a grandchild) later in life. Anger, depression, guilt, broken relationships, low self-esteem, sleep disorders, and a deep feeling of emptiness and loss can all follow an abortion.

Dealing with these emotions is difficult. There is no coffin or grave to visit to help ease the pain. Haunting emotional memories can last for years. Abortion may fix some temporary problems like embarrassment and inconvenience, but it causes many, many more.

Mother Teresa put it this way: "Abortion kills twice. It kills the body of the baby and the conscience of the mother." In order to dull the pain, the mother must learn to ignore the persistent prodding of her conscience.

According to a survey conducted by the *Los Angeles Times*, more than half the women who have abortions suffer from great guilt years later. And get this — more than *two thirds of the men who would have been fathers do too!*[1] It is a man's role to provide for and protect the life he has created. These are his God-given instincts. When he is denied that role, guilt often follows.

Preserving a pregnancy also protects from the physical complications of abortion, which occur close to ten percent of the time. Infection, bleeding, cervical or uterine damage, chronic abdominal pain, and increased chance of miscarriage are just a few of the more frequent complications.

Abortion is not just a simple procedure. It destroys the life and potential of the baby that is aborted. It robs the family of health and happiness. It affects the emotional and physical health of the mother and impacts the life of the father.

WHY IS IT SO HARD TO ACCEPT THIS STANDARD?

On January 22, 1973, the United States Supreme Court made a now-famous ruling in a case known as *Roe v. Wade.* Their ruling made abortions legal, and it changed American politics and family life forever.

Sides were immediately taken on the issue, and soon the sides were labeled. We continue to use the labels today. Those who accepted the court's decision and a woman's right to have an abortion are called "pro-choice." They adamantly fight for a woman's right to choose the fate of the fetus growing and developing inside her. Those who oppose the Supreme Court's decision on the basis that the object of abortion — the baby — is the handiwork of God are labeled "pro-life." They view the fetus as a life that deserves to be protected.

Pro-choice advocates offer several controversial arguments that sometimes cloud the vision of people trying to adopt a position on abortion. Let's talk about the most common ones.

If abortion is made illegal, millions of "unwanted" babies will be born and become the victims of child abuse and neglect. Statistics prove that legalizing abortion has not reduced child abuse at all. Instead, it seems to have reinforced the idea that only "wanted" children are valuable; therefore those who are "unwanted" can be extinguished or mistreated.

Also, this argument does not take into account the fact that an "unwanted" pregnancy does not necessarily result in an "unwanted" child. Many reluctant women have become loving, nurturing moms. And thousands of "wanting" homes are waiting to adopt otherwise "unwanted" children.

What about the baby that is going to be born into a life of poverty? It isn't fair to sentence a child and its mother to such a harsh life. Is it impossible for poor people to accomplish great things and find satisfaction in life? This statement seems to infer that poor people are not capable of enjoying life. Poverty is terrible, but to do away with anyone born into poverty would mean wiping out the majority of babies born in Africa, South America, Asia, and in countless homes throughout urban and rural America.

Many of the greatest contributions to our society have come from men and women who grew up in places of deep poverty and despair. Where would our society be without people like Abraham Lincoln, Mother Teresa, and Rosa Parks?

But what about the problem of overpopulation and the world hunger it causes? The number-one cause of hunger in the world today is war — not overpopulation — closely followed by political corruption and centralized economic control. If we want to solve the problem of world hunger, we need to work on these political problems first.

Or what about the baby that will be born with a defect? Is it fair to bring it into this world that idolizes perfection? The Bible tells us that God knows every detail of the body and life He is creating in the womb and that He loves each child He is forming. What often seems imperfect to us may be exactly what is best in His eyes.

Some very good friends of ours have a beautiful little Down's Syndrome daughter who has become the joy and delight of her family and friends. Raising a child with special needs is not easy, but it is transforming. It gives us a greater understanding of God's love for us. We have all been "handicapped" in some way by sin. God is not as interested in our physical or genetic perfection as He is in our moral condition.

What about the fact that if abortions are made illegal, women will be forced to have illegal, back-alley abortions like they did before the Supreme Court ruling? Many women will not get the medical treatment they need and some will die. The way to prevent women from dying is not by continuing the destruction of a million and a half babies every year. It is by offering pregnant women positive alternatives to abortion so that both the mother *and* the baby can go on living.

What about a woman whose life is threatened by pregnancy or childbirth? Shouldn't she have an abortion? Due to significant medical advances, it has become extremely rare for an abortion to be necessary to save a mother's life. But life-saving abortions were legal before *Roe v. Wade* and will continue to be legal even if other abortion is outlawed.

What if the pregnancy is due to a rape or incest? How could a pregnancy caused by such horrible circumstances possibly result in a blessing? First of all, let me mention that ninety-eight percent of all abortions are performed for reasons other than incest or rape.[2] And interestingly enough, studies show that 75 to 85 percent of rape victims who become pregnant choose not to have an abortion.[3] Therefore, very few abortions fit into this category.

Often in sexual assault cases, both the mother and child can be helped by preserving life rather than perpetuating violence. Some rape victims feel that they can conquer the awful act if they can get through the pregnancy. Finding the courage and strength it takes to make it through causes them to feel that they are better than the rapist. It allows them to be a survivor, not just a victim. It helps repair a self-esteem that could otherwise be shattered. The mothers-to-be in such cases seem to share the feeling that the life of that particular child may hold a very special significance. They acknowledge that God has a plan for their children's lives as well as for those conceived in a marriage relationship.

Ethel Waters, a famous jazz singer and actress, was conceived when her mother was raped. She grew up in extreme poverty, often having to steal food in order to eat. According to "pro-choice" reasoning, as a fetus she was an obvious candidate for abortion — twice! Yet her life and beautiful voice brought joy to thousands of people for many, many years.

Although most children of incest are aborted, incest victims rarely agree to these abortions of their own free will.[4] Most often they are "strongly encouraged" to terminate the pregnancy by the adults in their lives who convince them that it is "in their best interests." Yet the victim may see the pregnancy as a way out of the incestuous relationship. The birth of a baby will expose the horrible activity that has been secretly taking place — often over a long period of time. Sometimes the victim feels that if she has a baby, for the first time she will be able to establish a loving, reciprocal relationship. What is promoted as being done "in a girl's best interest" often isn't.

Every woman should have the right to choose whether or not she wants to have a baby. But, according to what I read in the Bible, she makes that choice and exercises that right completely when she chooses to engage in the sexual activity that causes a baby to be conceived. To abort an unwanted fetus is the equivalent of an airline pilot opening the hatch and kicking someone out of his plane at 35,000 feet. After he brings a passenger on board in Tampa, the captain can't suddenly change his mind and decide that he no longer wants that person to accompany him on the flight to Denver. That would be ludicrous!

The United States Supreme Court made a legal decision in 1973. But the United States Supreme Court is not infallible — as they proved in the nineteenth century when they ruled that a black man is only three-fifths of a human being in the eyes of the law. For them to rule that abortion is a *legal* right does not make it a *moral* right. Abortion destroys the life of a child created by God.

HOW CAN YOU LIVE UP TO GOD'S STANDARD?

The decisions you make concerning the abortion issue come down to whether or not you attribute as much value to the life of an unborn child as God does. God views the unborn child as just that — a *child* who is a distinct and valuable individual. It has a form that He is intricately involved in creating and a future that He is intimately involved in preparing. And He has entrusted its care to a particular mother and father. To do away with such a precious gift is to ignore God's standard of preserving life.

We must never ever look at pregnancy as a " situation" that needs to be resolved. It is a life that needs to be saved. One mistake or wrong decision cannot be undone by making another. It can only be compounded.

Tens of thousands of loving couples who cannot have children of their own are waiting to adopt the babies that will be born into homes unable to give them the love and nurture that they need. Most of these couples have to wait years before such a child is available. Some of them never receive a child, because abortion destroys so many millions of babies. Placing a baby in a loving home can be the best way of redeeming a less than ideal situation.

I pray that this is a decision you will never have to make, but if you do, just remember, it takes a hero to stand up for the life of an unborn child when everyone else around is calling for its destruction.

SUMMARY

A child in the womb is the handiwork of God and very precious to Him. To destroy an embryo or a fetus for any reason not only destroys the baby's life but wreaks havoc in the life of the intended mother and damages all those whose lives it was meant to bless.

Pro-choice arguments are not valid when measured by the truths found in the Bible and the statistics generated by our society. To place an otherwise "unwanted" baby up for adoption is a very valid and loving choice to make. Remember, a child who enters a womb has been invited. He or she is not an intruder.

DILEMMA #8

CAN'T I JUST SEE FOR MYSELF WHAT'S WRONG WITH DRUGS *and Alcohol? I Won't Become Addicted!*

WHEN ZACH WAS SMALL, WE BOUGHT A SHINY, BLACK, KID-SIZED MOTOR-cycle. It had no engine or pedals, but with sheer foot power, Zach could zoom that thing so fast I had to run to keep up with him. It was his favorite riding toy. Before Zach could outgrow it, MattE adopted it as *his* favorite mode of transportation — which not only created a few diplomatic dilemmas, it also meant that the little motorcycle was revving and rolling all day long.

A few years later, it was passed on to Ben. I believe that it must have been the sturdiest toy ever manufactured, because it was still in great condition when we moved to Lakeland, Florida, where Jonathan rode it up and down the driveway every day. That little black motorcycle soon became the hit of the new neighborhood. Other children constantly borrowed it and took it for a spin. Every evening it was the last toy put away on the back porch, and every morning it was the first one wheeled outside for play.

But one summer evening, as we put our toys away, we couldn't find the motorcycle. We searched everywhere. We finally gave up, figuring that one of our neighbors must have stashed it in his or her garage for safekeeping. We resumed our search the next morning, but our favorite toy didn't reappear.

It wasn't until the following spring, when the water level in the pond behind our house receded, that we finally discovered the motorcycle. It had spent a soggy fall and winter buried under the hyacinths near a neighbor's dock. It was rusted beyond repair.

We later found out that one of the children who lived near us had borrowed it — which he often did. But that day he had grown tired of riding it around the cul-de-sac and down the long driveway that had been designated for its use. So he had taken it across a neighbor's yard, along a dirt path, and up a steep embankment where he could coast down the other side into the shallow water of the pond. Several friends had joined him at this point, and they started a competition to see who could fly down the bank the fastest and land the farthest out in the water. It was a fun game — until the motorcycle became stuck in the muck at the bottom of the pond. At that point they abandoned it, and the motorcycle was left to deteriorate in the murky water.

I know this story brings tears to Jonathan's eyes (at least it did about fourteen years ago), but there's a reason I brought it up. It illustrates why it is wrong for us to do anything that is potentially abusive or destructive to our bodies.

The boy who borrowed the motorcycle was not wrong to do so. No, we had agreed that anyone could borrow it as long as he returned it later in the day. Paul (which is not his real name, because we never filled his parents in on the fact that he was the one who totaled our toy) was perfectly justified in using it anytime he wanted. But that motorcycle did not belong to him. What he did wrong was to take that little black motorcycle beyond the boundaries that we had set. If it had been his own (and if his mother had given him permission), he could have ridden it into the lake as often and as far as he liked.

But for safety reasons, we had set limits. The motorcycle was only to be ridden in the places we had designated. The areas were large and provided limitless opportunities for speed and experimentation. Banks along the driveway provided thrills (and sometimes spills). There were obstacles that could be placed in the cul-de-sac to assess ability and accuracy, and a quarter-mile loop around the long, circular drive that tested endurance. But Paul wanted more. So he took something that did not belong to him and used it in a way that not only caused its destruction, but that affected the playtime of at least half a dozen other children.

Using drugs, abusing alcohol, or participating in any activities that in any way destroy or addict our bodies is wrong for the same reasons. Our bodies are not our own. They belong to God, and for our safety He has set some very specific boundaries. We are obligated to abide by them.

WHAT IS GOD'S STANDARD REGARDING ABUSIVE, DESTRUCTIVE, AND ADDICTIVE BEHAVIORS?

Many people who lived in Corinth, and claimed to be Christians during the first century A.D., were notorious for pushing the limits and overstepping the boundaries that God had designed for them. In 1 Corinthians 6:19-20, an exasperated apostle Paul asks the Corinthians this question: "Do you not know that your body is a temple of the Holy Spirit, who is in you, whom you have received from God?" Then he explains to them, "You are not your own; you were bought at a price. Therefore honor God with your body."

Once we become Christians, our bodies do not belong to us. They belong to God, and He sends His Holy Spirit to live in them. To bring harm to our bodies in any way is to destroy something that we do not own. Paul put it this way: "Don't you know that you yourselves are God's temple and that God's Spirit lives in you? If anyone destroys God's temple, God will destroy him; for God's temple is sacred, and you are that temple" (1 Corinthians 3:16-17).

God has designed our bodies and lent them to us as very special containers that will carry our souls through life. The use of tobacco, alcohol, marijuana, cocaine, or any hallucinatory drug is not only against the law for teenagers, it is wrong because of the damage it can cause to God's property. The same goes for gluttony, or anorexia, or bulimia, or slashing, or anything else we could do to purposely harm our bodies.

Another boundary God set for us is not allowing our minds to be controlled by anything other than the Holy Spirit. In Matthew 22:37 Jesus tells us that the greatest commandment God ever gave us is to "love the Lord your God with all your heart and with all your soul and *with all your mind*" (emphasis added). If our rational thinking processes are under the control of delusional powers (induced by drugs or alcohol or even some meditative activities), it is impossible for us to love God the way we are supposed to.

Our minds are similar to the gasoline tanks in our cars. What we fill them with determines how well they will function. It would be a whole lot cheaper to fill our cars with water instead of gasoline, but that wouldn't get us very far. Cars weren't designed to operate that way. As a matter of fact, water in a carburetor will ruin it completely.

Ephesians 5:18-20 says that our lives are to be filled and controlled by the Holy Spirit. His power filling our minds should affect our actions, our habits, and our desires in a positive way every bit as much as filling our minds with alcohol or drugs affects them in a negative way. Our joy and exhilaration and comfort and peace are to come from the Holy Spirit. Any other substitute will not get us where God wants us to be. We become as useless as a car with a wet carburetor.

God created everything on this planet, including the ingredients for wine and alcohol and the drugs we formulate. Psalm 104:14-15 says, "(God) makes grass grow for the cattle, and plants for man to cultivate — bringing forth food from the earth: wine that gladdens the heart of man, oil to make his face shine, and bread that sustains his heart." But it has always been our duty to subdue and bring the things on this earth into compliance with God's standards (see Genesis 1:28).

Alcohol in and of itself is not evil. In fact, in His first recorded miracle, Jesus turned water into wine at a wedding in Cana of Galilee (see John 2). However, allowing oneself to be under the control of wine or alcohol *is* wrong. Ephesians 5:18 plainly states, "Do not get drunk on wine."

Proverbs 23:29-35 describes the scary situation many people find themselves in when they allow alcohol to enter their lives:

> Who has woe? Who has sorrow? Who has strife? Who
> has complaints? Who has needless bruises? Who has
> bloodshot eyes? Those who linger over wine, who go
> to sample bowls of mixed wine. Do not gaze at wine
> when it is red, when it sparkles in the cup, when it
> goes down smoothly! In the end it bites like a snake
> and poisons like a viper. Your eyes will see strange
> sights and your mind imagine confusing things. You
> will be like one sleeping on the high seas, lying on
> top of the rigging. "They hit me," you will say, "but I'm

not hurt! They beat me, but I don't feel it! When will I wake up so I can find another drink?"

People have no way of knowing whether or not they will become addicted when they first use alcohol, cigarettes, marijuana, or any other drug. Addiction is no respecter of persons — rich or poor, black or white, smart or dumb, churched or unchurched — everyone is vulnerable. Although some cases of alcoholism and other addictions might stem from genetic tendencies and may even be categorized as illnesses, they are not excusable. God has warned us to stay away from the triggers that would cause them to surface in our lives.

WHY DID GOD DESIGN THIS STANDARD?

God did not just look around His creation one day and say, "Hmmm. I'm going to take a little fun away from the people on my planet. I think I'll make it a no-no for them to use alcohol or marijuana or any of the other drugs that can give them a sensation of pleasure or numb the awareness of pain in their lives." No, God's purpose in setting such things off-limits was to protect us from the havoc that they can wreak in our lives.

1. Staying away from drugs and alcohol protects us from their downward spiral of destruction and allows us to achieve our goals.

I know that each of you has goals, things that you want to accomplish in life. But unless the lifestyle you are living is leading you in their direction, you will never reach them. Everything you do either directs you closer to your goals or takes you further away from them. And once you start heading in the wrong direction, it is very hard to get back on track.

Several years ago we went skiing in Colorado. Three of my

goals were to have fun, not to get hurt, and to be able to ski better when I left than when I arrived. By the end of the second day I was feeling pretty good about my accomplishments. I was learning to sit back on my skis, bend my knees, and zigzag down the mountain with the best of them — at least the ones who were still traversing the green slopes.

By the third day I was doing so well that I decided to attempt a blue slope. It was much more difficult than I had anticipated, but I did okay — until, somehow, I got off course and found myself going over the edge of a black diamond!

Once I started down, there was no way to go back up. I was trapped into going in a totally different direction than I had intended. About halfway to the bottom, I took off my skis and trudged down the remainder of the mountain. Even that was difficult in the waist-deep powder! Needless to say, I accomplished none of my goals that day.

If you decide to experiment with alcohol or tobacco or drugs, you are likely to find yourself on the back side of a very slippery mountain heading in the opposite direction from your goals and dreams.

Do you think the young man who went to a party with his buddies and drank beer for the first time intended to become the mean alcoholic who terrorizes his family, making his children fear him and his wife despise him? Do you think the athlete who chewed tobacco to while away the time in the dugout ever anticipated the massive medical bills or the trauma that accompanied the cancer he acquired? Do you think the pretty cheerleader who was always the life of the party purposely got hooked on drugs and wound up in some hellhole wishing she had the guts to take her own life?

What about the peer-pleasing teenager who had a couple of beers at a friend's house just to feel accepted? Do you think he or she meant to cause the accident that claimed the life of a friend and crippled a young child for life? (Did you know that alcohol and related highway accidents are the number-one killer of fifteen- to twenty-four-year-olds?)

No, each of these people had goals and dreams that were shattered by the very thing that was supposed to bring joy, or relieve stress, or boost popularity.

Experimentation almost always leads to association with those who are regularly involved in substance abuse. This association invariably leads to further abuse and eventually winds up in dependency and addiction. In the process, moral values deteriorate and old friendships are sacrificed. Lifelong goals are set aside in pursuit of momentary pleasures.

The spiral keeps going down. Because of the consequences of strained family relationships or the personal crises that develop, feelings of being abandoned by God typically follow, which can lead to anger and separation from Him. A distorted, stuporlike consciousness takes the place of real spiritual experience.

God knows what devastation addictive substances can bring into our lives. He wants to help us *cope* with our problems, not *compound* them. That's why He warns us to stay away from drugs and alcohol and any other substances or behaviors that can take over the control of our minds and our bodies. They were designed to function best with the Holy Spirit filling and controlling them.

2. Staying away from drugs and alcohol protects us from damaging relationships and preserves our credibility.

All excesses and addictions become family affairs. None of us lives in isolation. Just as the destruction of a toy motorcycle affected the pleasure of many neighborhood children, all of our actions touch the people whose lives surround ours.

Although the abuse of drugs was not the cultural issue during biblical times that it is today, drunkenness was an issue. And whenever it is mentioned in the Bible, drunkenness is condemned. That's because drunkenness destroys credibility. It caused Noah to act shamefully (see Genesis 9:20-21) and Lot to engage in incestuous activity (see Genesis 19:30-36). It destroyed Belshazzar's kingdom and stripped him of all his dignity (see Daniel 5). Drunkenness cost Nabal (see 1 Samuel 25:36-37) and Elah (see 1 Kings 16:9-10) and some of the Corinthians (see 1 Corinthians 11:21-31) their lives. First Corinthians 5:11 tells us that we are not even supposed to associate with or eat with people who claim to be Christians and are drunkards.

Drunkenness not only destroys credibility, it disqualifies people from positions of authority. First Timothy 3:3,8 and Titus 1:7 tell us that people who indulge in wine should not be allowed to become leaders in the church.

Drunkenness and drugs also open our minds to deception. When we give up the control of our minds, we are easily manipulated by outside forces. We can be led to trust people and embrace philosophies that we would certainly reject if the Holy Spirit were controlling our reactions and responses.

WHY IS IT SO HARD TO ACCEPT THIS STANDARD?

More than anything else, the desire for peer approval and acceptance is what motivates teenagers to disregard God's instructions and to experiment with substances and activities that are inconsistent with His standards. The fear of being left on the "out-side" of the "in-crowd" is difficult to accept. And the in-crowd these days seems to be seeking its own pleasure regardless of the laws of God or society. When faced with a room full of cheering or jeering peers, it is hard for anyone to cling to the truth that God's approval is all that really counts.

The media reinforces the idea that "everyone" who is cool is engaging in addictive and abusive behaviors. In a distortion of reality, they depict a wonderful world where everyone is partying and drinking or doing drugs and having a fabulous time. Beer advertisements show sophisticated, successful, popular people (and sometimes even amphibians!) enjoying the "benefits" of a "cold one." In sit-coms and movies, clean-living kids are almost always categorized as dorks. They are portrayed as the exception — especially when it comes to alcohol use. It is a message that is hard to ignore.

Some teenagers find themselves turning to abusive or addictive behavior to numb the pain in their lives — the ache of rejection or the fear of failure. Feelings of inadequacy or shyness seem to vanish under the influence of mind-controlling substances. Instead of taking their hurts and fears and inadequacies to God (see 1 Peter 5:7), some of your friends search for a false reservoir of strength and invulnerability through drugs and alcohol.

Others experiment with drugs or alcohol for the sheer thrill of the experience. Our human nature seems to be magnetized to the excitement and intrigue of doing something that is wrong and trying to get away with it. Breaking the law, whether society's or God's, produces a false sense of power. The first few times a person experiments with drugs or alcohol may be big on thrills and small on consequences, but by the time he or she experiences the downside to these mind-controlling substances, many teenagers find themselves trapped.

HOW CAN YOU LIVE UP TO GOD'S STANDARD?

Every day thousands of teenagers risk their futures, the safety of others, and even their own lives by allowing the opinions of others to be more important than the assessment of God. Good kids find themselves unable to make wise decisions, their minds paralyzed by peer pressure. And the cost of giving in to such pressure is often measured in tragic ways. The abusive and addictive behaviors that follow can result in missed opportunities, wasted lives, prison sentences, spiritual bankruptcy, and a multitude of other heartbreaking catastrophes.

You must determine to stay away from the people who seek to find fulfillment or excitement in things that are abusive and destructive, no matter how nerdy they may say you are.

You must make every effort to avoid the places where such actions are acceptable, no matter how left out you may feel.

You must decide ahead of time that you will not remain in any situation that could influence you to take part in such activities. If you resolve right now that you will never attend a party that is not chaperoned by adults, it will be very helpful later on. It is not safe to trust the other teenagers involved in such situations to make wise decisions regarding the opportunities that present themselves. (And be aware that not all adults make wise decisions either. I know of several parties in the last few months where parents either supplied alcohol or looked the other way while their teenagers raided the liquor cabinet. It is always wise to have an escape plan just in case such a situation occurs. Whatever it takes to get out of there, you must not stick around!)

You must never fool yourself into thinking that you are strong enough or wise enough to remain unaffected. To say, "Nothing will happen to me. I can handle it," is to mock God and pretend you are wiser than He is. Galatians 6:7-8 tells us the results of such self-deception: "Do not be deceived. God cannot be mocked. A man reaps what he sows. The one who sows to please his sinful nature, from that nature will reap destruction; the one who sows to please the Spirit, from the Spirit will reap eternal life." You can expect that it will be a struggle to live up to these ideals. But you can also expect God to honor you for making choices that honor Him.

As well as making these promises to yourself before God, it is important for you to find friends who will support your decisions and hold you accountable to them. Peer pressure is the most influential factor in a teenager's life, and *it does not always have to be negative!* In fact, it can be very helpful if those peers are headed in the same direction and reaching for the same goals that you are. Let me tell you a story about peer pressure.

In the middle of the Depression, Sylvan Goldman, an Oklahoma grocer, bought several bankrupt Humpty Dumpty stores. He figured that even in bad times people had to eat. Despite that truth, he soon found himself in deep financial trouble.

Goldman began to watch his shoppers closely, looking for ways to capitalize on their habits. He noticed that they headed to the cashier whenever their hand-held baskets became heavy. That put an end to their shopping experience, because once they had checked out they did not reenter the store. So, in 1936, he designed a carriage made out of a folding chair. He attached wheels to it, then fitted two metal baskets inside. He figured that if he could design a way to take weight out of the shopping experience, maybe his customers would buy more items.

He was wrong. No one wanted anything to do with the contraptions, and they continued to carry their baskets to the cashiers whenever they were heavy. But Goldman did not give up. He actually hired people to wheel the new carts around. He made sure that several smiling "fake" customers walked back and forth near the entrance pushing carts loaded with groceries. Then he placed someone at the front door to offer real customers the new contraptions as they walked in. Sure enough, people started using the carts and quickly began to prefer them.

At his death, Sylvan Goldman left behind over 400 million dollars, much of it due to his invention of the shopping cart — an invention that never would have worked had not peer pressure been applied to help pull it off.

We need to be sure that we have people in our lives who will exert positive peer pressure, people who will help us see the value of taking care of our bodies according to God's standards.

SUMMARY

The bottom line is this — when you are searching for joy, exhilaration, comfort, and peace, you must know where to find them. The Holy Spirit is the only One who can give these things to you. They cannot be found in friends or fads or mind-controlling substances. Abusive and addictive behaviors can only distance you from them. Anything else that pretends to offer them only provides a false substitute. The freedom they seem to offer actually leads to a life of domination and slavery.

When problems arise in your life, determine that you will face them with the help of others, rather than try to escape from them. Spend time in the Bible reading how people in similar situations found their refuge and strength in God. Let the Holy Spirit be your comforter and guide as Jesus promised He would be (see John 14:25-27). God wants your mind to be free and clear to love and worship Him.

If you've already blown it and find yourself chained to behaviors that you know are wrong, remember, the Holy Spirit can bring healing in your life. He is stronger than any of the powers in this world (see 1 John 4:4). You need to admit to Him (and to yourself) that what you are doing is wrong. You must allow Him, and the people who love you, to help. You cannot overcome an addiction on your own. You need to find Christian counselors and true friends who want to help you succeed. You must ask God to change your desires and then trust Him to change you into the whole, beautiful person that He intended you to be. Only then can "the God of hope fill you with all joy and peace as you trust in him, so that you may overflow with hope by the power of the Holy Spirit" (Romans 15:13).

A test of sobriety often given by police officers involves checking your ability to walk in a straight line. It is good every once in a while to stop and check how straight you are walking in your relationship with God. Are you able to love Him with *all* your mind?

DILEMMA #9

WHY ARE YOU SO CONCERNED ABOUT OUR MUSIC, MODEMS, and the Media? It's Only Entertainment!

WHEN I WAS GROWING UP, I WAS NOT ALLOWED TO GO ON AN UNACCOM-panied date until I turned sixteen. For the most part, this restriction didn't cause me much concern. I was part of a group of teenagers who hung out and did everything together. We really didn't need dates to have a good time. Bowling, or going to a football game, or ice skating on the lake behind my best friend's house were much more fun when there were lots of kids around.

But four months before I turned sixteen, I noticed Bill — and, believe it or not, Bill noticed me! He was a senior and the presi-dent of the student body at a large city high school several miles away. I was a sophomore without much claim to fame at a small rural high school. Soon, going to ice-skating parties and attending sporting events took on a whole new interest for me.

I'll never forget the phone conversation when Bill asked if I would like to go with him to a college basketball game. It was the first date I had ever been asked to go on. I didn't know how to reply. I didn't want to tell him I couldn't go unless someone else came along, but I knew I couldn't lie or sneak off without telling my parents.

Finally, after two absurdly silent minutes during which my mind raced in frenzied circles, I blurted out, "I'd love to go with you, but can we take Drew along?" Drew was my younger brother. It was probably the dumbest suggestion I ever made in my life, but it was the best plan I could come up with at the moment.

So sure enough, that Friday evening Bill picked me *and* Drew up and took us *both* to the basketball game. Drew couldn't seem to grasp the idea that he was just along for the ride and should make himself as invisible as possible. He stuck by our sides every second of that date! He leaned over the front seat of the car on the way to the game so that he could take part in our conversation. He sat right next to us in the arena even though there were tons of empty seats. He accompanied us to the concession stand every time we went. The only time he left us alone was when Bill bribed him with a dollar to dump our trash in the hallway outside the arena. The excursion took him a grand total of three minutes!

I was shocked when Bill asked me out again. I was determined to come up with a better solution than to drag Drew along. But at the last second my solution fell through, and Drew went ice skating with us.

As you can imagine, my relationship with Bill did not progress very far. After two months of dating me (*and* Drew), Bill decided to find someone a little less encumbered. I couldn't blame him.

I couldn't decide whether I should love or hate my little brother. Without his presence, I probably wouldn't have been able to date Bill at all. Yet many times I wished he would go away and never come back. There were a lot of things that Bill and I were not free to experience in our dating relationship as long as my little brother was there gawking at us with his big, innocent eyes.

Believe it or not, there is a Drew in your life right now — and at times His presence can seem just as annoying! In the last chapter, we talked about the Holy Spirit and how He comes to live inside every person who accepts the sacrifice that Jesus Christ made on the cross. Our bodies actually become His dwelling place (see 1 Corinthians 6:19). Do you know what that means?

That means *everywhere* we go in life, He comes along! Everything we see in life, He sees. Everything we do in life, we do in His presence. There is not a single thing we can bribe Him with to make Him go away. (And I thought Drew was a pest!)

That means the Holy Spirit sits through every movie and television program we watch. He reads every magazine or book we read. He views every e-mail and instant message we receive. He sees every Internet site that we open. And He listens to every word of every lyric of every CD we play. And sometimes He's not very happy! Ephesians 4:30 tells us that some of the things we do actually *grieve* the Holy Spirit.

A struggle exists because we live in a world filled with sin. Jesus tells us that although we are living *in* the world, we are not to be *of* the world (see John 17:14-18). He doesn't ask us to withdraw from society and live monastic lives away from its temptations and turmoil. Nor does He want us to go to the opposite extreme and carelessly abandon ourselves to the pleasures of our culture. God wants us to live according to His standards *while* we struggle to maintain a redeeming relationship with the world.

WHAT IS GOD'S STANDARD REGARDING MUSIC, MODEMS, AND THE MEDIA?

In the last chapter we discovered that God wants each of us to love Him with all our heart and with all our soul and *with all our mind* (see Matthew 22:37). We discussed how our minds must be *clear* if we are to worship Him the way we are supposed to. They must be available to be influenced by the Holy Spirit, never clouded or controlled by another substance or activity.

Our minds must not only be *clear*, they must be *clean* and *uncluttered* as well. In Philippians 4:8, God describes what types of things we should allow to occupy our minds: "Whatever is true, whatever is noble, whatever is right, whatever is pure, whatever is lovely, whatever is admirable — if anything is excellent or praiseworthy — think about such things."

You know as well as I do that most of the movies, the majority of television shows, the bulk of teen magazines, the lyrics to many contemporary songs, and an incredible number of Internet sites could not be described by God's list of acceptable adjectives. Therefore the thought processes they produce cannot be God-pleasing, nor the dirty residue they leave behind praiseworthy or excellent. And the space they take up in our minds is completely wasted.

God's standard for our use of music, modems, and the media is very simple and direct. Every time we watch a movie or a television show; every time we pick up a magazine or listen to a CD or sign on to the Internet, we must ask ourselves: *Is what I am allowing to enter my mind true, noble, right, pure, lovely,* and *admirable? Would God agree that what I am looking at is excellent? Is the Holy Spirit praising me for what I am allowing Him to hear?*

WHY DID GOD DESIGN THIS STANDARD?

Did you know that after you accept Jesus as your Savior, the Holy Spirit not only comes to live in your life and to accompany you everywhere you go, but that He sets up His office in your mind? It becomes His workshop. It is where He carries out the assignments He has been given in your life.

From His office space in our minds, the Holy Spirit runs a multitask operation. He provides us with services such as "teaching" and "guiding" and "reminding" so that we can understand the Bible and appreciate God's perspective in every situation that we encounter. He also manufactures some very special products in our lives. Among them are love, joy, peace, and patience (see Galatians 5:22-23).

But we have a very important role in the daily operation of His business. We are the *custodians,* and as such it is our job to keep the workspace clean and tidy. It is amazing how efficient the Holy Spirit can be when His workspace is clear and clean and uncluttered. But as soon as things get messy, His productivity slows considerably. He cannot perform His valuable tasks or produce his priceless products in the filth and fog of a messed-up mind.

Ben has a big English paper in his bedroom that he has been working on for several days. I wonder what he would do if one of his brothers came into his room tonight and messed everything up. Suppose that brother (probably the youngest one) spread magazines and CDs and gum wrappers all over his desk, then left a leaky soda can on top of it all.

When Ben walked in and discovered that his paper was all crumpled and sticky, he would be very upset, wouldn't he? That's putting it mildly! He would make his slovenly brother clear off all the junk so that he could have his workspace back. He'd supervise him while he cleaned up every drop of soda and wiped away every smidgen of stickiness. And he'd probably make him retype the paper — including the bibliography, which he hasn't even begun! But the point is this — he needs his desk to be clean and uncluttered in order to finish his project.

When we allow our minds to absorb the trivia and trash so prevalent in today's entertainment world, we allow the workspace of the Holy Spirit to become cluttered with useless junk, and we let it get sticky from the filthy residue. His progress is hindered and, therefore, our lives are damaged.

We must do anything we can to keep our minds clear and clean and uncluttered so that the Holy Spirit can perform his valuable services and fill our lives with his wonderful products.

1. Having uncluttered minds allows us to experience the fruit of the Holy Spirit. This will make us contented people in a discontented society.

Galatians 5:22-23 tells us that the Holy Spirit wants to fill our lives with "love, joy, peace, patience, kindness, goodness, faithfulness, gentleness and self-control." Think about it — aren't these the qualities of life that most people in our society are desperately trying to achieve? Aren't these the characteristics that *you* really want in *your* life? I know I want them in mine! Well, they are the by-products of a mind that loves God completely.

But ever since sin wiggled its ugly way onto this planet, a tug of war for our loyalty has ensued. And the battle takes place in our minds. The bottom line is: whom will we choose to love and worship, God or the things of this world? Satan is wise enough to understand that we don't have to bow down and worship *him* in order for his side to win the battle and capture our allegiance. All he has to do is get us to ignore God.

Satan uses media, music, and the other devices of this world to lure our thoughts away from God. He is making an all-out effort to captivate our minds with worthless facts and fantasies, and fill them up with useless information so that we do not have the time to think of God or any room for His Holy Spirit to work.

When our minds are subject to the constant, selfish cravings that the media stirs up, we find it hard to be content. There are always bigger, better, louder, smoother, sexier, smarter "whatevers" that we find ourselves wanting to own or do. Discontentment is like a cancer that keeps us from enjoying life. It robs us of satisfaction and peace. It eats away at our relationships and eventually leads to loneliness.

But when we expose our minds only to things that are pleasing to the Holy Spirit (the things described in Philippians 4:8), we can't be trapped by Satan's strategy. Our minds cannot be saturated by the self-centered, self-promoting philosophy of the media. They cannot be lured into lustful dissatisfaction or chronic disappointment. They are free to worship God and enjoy the benefits of His Holy Spirit. A life that is full of love and joy and peace and patience and kindness and goodness and faithfulness and gentleness and self-control is a life that is content.

2. Having clean minds makes it possible for us to respond to God's love without any guilt or shame.

According to 1 John 2:15-16, "If anyone loves the world, the love of the Father is not in him. For everything in the world — the cravings of sinful man, the lust of his eyes and the boasting of what he has and does — comes not from the Father but from the world."

When we allow ourselves to watch questionable scenes on TV or expose ourselves to risqué descriptions in magazines or books; when we revel in the ruthless violence of a video game or gawk at lewd pictures on the Internet; when we let the vulgar lyrics of a CD or the unwholesome message of a popular movie run through our minds, we are violating God's requirement to keep our minds clean and pure. We are being lousy custodians! These activities make it impossible for the Holy Spirit to do His work and for us to love God with every part of our minds. This disappoints

God and brings guilt and shame into our lives.

Many years ago your Aunt Nino gave me a very special music box. It was a little, square chapel with a tall, white steeple. Every time I wound it up, the wooden doors opened and closed and a little preacher man in a black suit waddled in and out as it played *Amazing Grace*. But one day, when Jonathan was four years old, his curiosity took over. He investigated the technology that made it work, and ended up destroying my music box. I told you about this in the book *Sticking Up for What I Believe* (question #4). But I didn't tell you how he reacted after he broke it.

Jonathan placed my music box back on the shelf in exactly the same place that I always kept it. He stuffed the disconnected wires and the pulleys and the little preacher man inside the chapel and closed the doors. Then for several hours he avoided me. He didn't want to help me bake chocolate chip cookies. He didn't want to play Monopoly with me, even though it was his favorite game. He wasn't even excited about going to Baskin-Robbins for ice cream. I couldn't figure out what was wrong with him.

Finally, Jonathan couldn't stand the tension any longer. During dinner he blurted out that he had broken my music box, and he brought it to me with tear-filled eyes. I hugged him and forgave him and he promised to buy me another one when he got bigger. (I'm still waiting!) But the guilt that had kept us apart was gone. We were able to enjoy each other's company again.

Guilt always causes relationships to deteriorate. It causes us to distance ourselves from the people we want to love. This distance places a strain on the bonds that hold us together.

We must realize that it is never God who withdraws His love and creates the tension between us. He never changes. His arms are always outstretched, waiting for us to return, no matter how far we pull away. When we clear away the clutter and scour the sticky filth from our minds, the Holy Spirit is free to guide us into understanding and experiencing the completeness of God's unchanging love. Then we will want to begin to use the music, modems, and media in our world in ways that will bring us closer to God.

WHY IS IT SO HARD TO ACCEPT THIS STANDARD?

Satan has made it very difficult for us to keep the Holy Spirit's workshop clean. We are exposed to a daily diet of lyrics and images and philosophical statements that blur the distinction between right and wrong and show no consequences for ungodly choices. Let me ask you a question. Of all the characters you've seen on television who have had either an open or implied sexual relationship, how many of them have also been shown to contract an STD or have to deal with an unplanned pregnancy? Not very many, right?

Most television shows and movies accept sexual immorality and violence as the social norm. Why? Because it sells! And our society is driven by commercialism. But what they are selling is an unrealistic, untruthful version of immorality. It lures us with false beauty, hollow promises, temporary pleasures, and counterfeit wisdom. And it results in deadly decisions.

What would have been in the bottom of a trashcan twenty years ago is on the top of the charts today. What is rated PG for content today would have been rated R a few years ago. God's standards have not changed, and they never will. But because of the extreme overexposure, our consciences have been dulled.

The more we are exposed to something, the more likely we are to engage in it. Oh, we might be prideful and careless enough to think that we won't let the things that surround us influence us, but exposure destroys our "sex-immune systems" and tears down our "violence-control panels." Whether we realize it or not, we are being conditioned to derive pleasure from immoral sex and uncontrolled violence.

Unwilling to stand up against the pressure, or reluctant to recognize the danger, we find ourselves tagging along to movies that we know we shouldn't see or listening to music we know we shouldn't hear. And we wind up sabotaging the Holy Spirit's workspace, leaving a messy grime all over the peace and joy He was preparing just for us.

HOW CAN WE LIVE UP TO GOD'S STANDARD?

Second Corinthians 10:5 tells us that we are to "take captive every thought to make it obedient to Christ." We can't keep every wrong thought or impulse or emotion from showing up at the door to the Holy Spirit's hangout. Thoughts are like packages that are dropped off on the doorstep by the mailman. But it is our job, as custodians, to decide whether or not to accept them and take them inside.

Every thought we allow must be able to pass the eight-question test in Philippians 4:8. (If you think I'm being redundant, trust me, I am! I want you to understand the importance of asking yourself these questions.)

1. Is this thought *true?* Does it encourage me to live up to the standards God has designed for my life?
2. Is it *noble?* Does it increase my desire to honor God?
3. Is it *right?* Does it help me to be honest and completely innocent in God's eyes?
4. Is it *pure?* Is it clean enough that I can dedicate it to God?
5. Is it *lovely?* Is it so pleasing that it compels me to love God even more?
6. Is it *admirable?* Would God respect it?

7. Is it *excellent?* Is it the very best thought I could have about this object or subject?
8. Is it *worthy of praise?* Would God congratulate me for having it?

The quickest way to frisk a thought is to ask ourselves: Would Jesus have allowed this thought to enter His mind? If not, we should not allow it to enter ours either! We must turn away every unacceptable thought.

The best way to keep wrong thoughts from threatening the thresholds of our minds is to stay away from the people and places that can cause us to have them. After years of being a school nurse and watching illness and epidemics spread through the various schools I serviced, I discovered an astounding principle: *Disease is easily transmitted. Wellness is not!* Think about it. If Dad had the flu and I was perfectly well and we kissed each other, what would happen? Would he get better? No! More than likely I would get sick. His illness could easily be transmitted to me, but my wellness could not be transmitted to him.

This same medical principle applies to morality and righteousness. Sinful habits and behaviors are easily transmitted, but righteousness is not.

The Bible confirms this. In Haggai 2:11-14 (paraphrased), the prophet asks the priests this question: "If one of you carries a consecrated piece of meat in his pocket, and that pocket touches some other food, does the holiness transfer to the bread or stew or wine or whatever was just touched by the garment?"

"No way," the priests reply.

"Well, then," Haggai asks them, "if a person who has been defiled by touching a dead body touches some food, does the food become defiled?"

They don't hesitate for a moment. "Absolutely!" they respond.

Haggai makes the point that proximity cannot purify something, but it certainly can defile it. The same is true when it comes to our thought life. We can't "catch" righteousness just from hanging around righteous people in righteous places. We have to ask Jesus Christ to cleanse us and renew our minds for that to take place. But it sure is easy for our thoughts to become impure when we let them wander into impure places!

Let me challenge you to keep a "music, modem, and media" journal for one day. In the first column, keep track of the music you listen to; list everything you watch on TV or at the movies; write down everything you read for pleasure; and record the sites you go to on the Internet. In the second column, record how many minutes you spend involved in each activity. In the third column, put a plus sign, a minus sign, or a zero beside each pastime you have listed. A plus sign means that the activity only allowed thoughts to enter your mind that would cause you to love God more. A minus sign means that the thoughts it created made the Holy Spirit's workshop cluttered or unclean. A zero means it had no effect either way. (Hmmm. It might be wise to go back and evaluate some of these again.) If you aren't sure how to grade an activity, evaluate the thoughts that the activity stimulated according to the eight-question test found in Philippians 4:8. If it does not pass *every one* of the questions, guess what? It gets a minus sign!

How uncluttered are you keeping the Holy Spirit's workshop? Do you truly love God with *all* your mind? Are you abiding by God's standards for your life when it comes to music, modems, and the media? This is not an issue you need to debate with your parents (although they may give you some very wise counsel). This is something you need to get right with God.

SUMMARY

The Holy Spirit not only enters our lives and accompanies us everywhere we go once we become Christians, He sets up shop in our minds. It is there that He provides valuable insights and direction. It is there that He produces the "fruit of the Spirit" mentioned in Galatians 5:22-23. It is our job to keep His work-space uncluttered and clean. This is impossible if we are allowing our minds to be exposed to the trivia and trash so prevalent in the music, modems, and media of our society.

In Philippians 4:8, God has provided us with very clear guidelines to evaluate each thought that tries to enter our minds. If the CDs, television shows, movies, reading material, Internet sites, and video games we view and listen to are not producing thoughts that are true, noble, right, pure, lovely, admirable, excellent, and worthy of praise, we need to eliminate them from our lives.

DILEMMA #10

WHAT IF I'VE ALREADY
Blown It?

A TINY FIRST-GRADER, DRIPPING WITH THE PERSPIRATION OF FEAR, SAT ALL alone on top of a high, stone wall which formed an imposing barricade and segregated her life from the world beyond. The little girl was a student at a boarding school in Africa, miles away from where her parents worked among the natives from primitive tribes. The wall formed a protective boundary between the school and the unforgiving African terrain. It ran the full length of the dining hall and wound its way somewhere beyond the tennis courts.

School rules demanded that no students be allowed anywhere near the wall, let alone to climb it! Word among the kids was that no one, except for one big eighth-grade guy named Grinder, had ever climbed to the top and lived to tell his tale. So how did a first-grade girl find herself straddling it at its highest point?

It was a mixture of an adventuresome curiosity, a peer challenge, and a very bad choice. I know — because I was that little girl!

As a six-year-old who had already faced numerous challenges in life, I wasn't about to let this one slip by. Day after day I sat staring across the campus at that wall. I knew that someday I *had* to climb it!

One afternoon, when no one else was around, I decided to try. I was only going to climb a little way up — just for practice to see if I could do it. But before I knew it, I was on top, straddling the stone wall and peering into the forbidden world that had only existed in my dreams.

But all that I could see (and smell!) as I gazed from my perch was a huge, filthy pigpen that filled the valley below. This was not what I had anticipated. My knees were scratched and bleeding from the climb, my body was trembling from the height, and no one was even around to share my victory. Arriving at the top of the wall quickly became a huge disappointment, which nearly turned into a disaster when I realized that there was no way down.

The dinner bell rang. My stomach growled. And my only hope for survival was to jump. So I did!

Splattered on the ground behind the dining hall, I slowly moved one finger, then another, then a leg, and finally I sat up. I was alive! I limped into the dining hall just in time for dessert.

When my dorm mother questioned my tardiness and examined my bloody knees, I mumbled something about falling down. I couldn't look her in the eye for weeks. I didn't want her to discover the truth. I knew she would be very disappointed in me — and that punishment was likely. I never went near that wall again.

WHEN WE IGNORE GOD'S STANDARDS, THERE ARE CONSEQUENCES

Every decision we make has consequences. When we make good choices, the consequences can be wonderful. However, when we make bad ones, they can be disastrous. As a first-grader, I decided that self-gratification and peer praise were more important to me than accepting the standards of the school administration. My choice left me hungry and hurting and hollow. No one believed that I had really climbed to the top of the wall, and I wasn't about to try it again. Fortunately, the consequences of my choice were not severe enough to maim me for life, but they were harsh enough to keep me from wanting to disobey the rules again.

God often allows us to experience the painful consequences of our choices, so that we will want to return to Him and enjoy the fellowship of being part of His family. You see, when we accept God's gift of salvation through Jesus Christ, we become His children. We maintain that relationship with Him for eternity! Nothing can ever alter it. Nothing that happens to us, no place we decide to go, nothing we choose to do can jeopardize our status as sons and daughters of the King of the Universe.

Paul expressed it this way: "For I am convinced that neither death nor life, neither angels nor demons, neither the present nor the future, nor any powers, neither height nor depth, nor *anything* else in all creation, will be able to separate us from the love of God that is in Christ Jesus our Lord" (Romans 8:38-39, emphasis added). Our choice to accept Jesus as our Savior results in a relationship with God that is unchangeable and eternal.

However, even though our *relationship* with God is eternally intact, our *fellowship* with Him can fluctuate. When I chose to disobey the school rules, it didn't change my status. I was still a child under the care and supervision of a wonderful dorm mother. But it greatly affected my fellowship with her. I was not free to enjoy her companionship or presence in my life for several weeks. I felt guilty for having disobeyed her, yet I began to resent the rules she represented.

When we choose to disobey or ignore God's standards, our companionship with Him can become very strained and His presence in our lives can grow quite awkward. As we distance ourselves from Him, our perspective of His love can become very

145

distorted. Because we are no longer willing to "look Him in the eyes," we can easily picture Him as imposing and mean and wanting revenge. We forget that He is our heavenly Father who lovingly wants to correct us. He wants to help us live up to His standards so that we can experience all the joys of being His children.

When we violate His standards, not only do we distance ourselves from God, but we can destroy our confidence and feelings of value as well. As we experience guilt and depression, we can begin to feel unworthy of His loving presence and doomed for failure. If we choose to continue in our sin, we can do great damage to our conscience. What was once a bad choice can become a habit, and we can eventually lose the ability to distinguish between right and wrong. But no matter how low it may take us, the downward spiral of sin in our lives does not have to continue.

WHEN WE ACKNOWLEDGE OUR SIN, GOD OFFERS US FORGIVENESS

For months Uncle Rick had a stomach ache, but was reluctant to admit the problem. Finally, when the pain became too severe for him to stand up straight, he went to the doctor. Sure enough, his appendix had burst, and he ended up in the operating room. It wasn't until he was willing to admit that he had a problem that the doctor could cure him — and he almost waited too long!

God has a cure for our sin problems, but He cannot apply His cure until we are willing to admit that we have violated His standards. First John 1:9 tells us, "If we confess our sins, he is faithful and just and will forgive us our sins." The word *confess* means to "agree with." When our heart agrees with God that we have sinned by violating His standards, He promises that He will forgive us.

In Psalm 103:3, David (who violated several of God's standards during his lifetime) praises God for the forgiveness he has experienced in his life. Full of thanksgiving he said, "He forgives *all* (my) sins and heals *all* (my) diseases" (emphasis added).

No matter how long or how hard you look, you will never find a clause in God's forgiveness contract that excludes any sins. God's forgiveness is complete and unconditional. We don't have to earn it or prove that we're worthy of it in any way. We just have to agree with Him that we need it.

Ephesians 2:1-7 is an incredible passage that tells us how much God loved us even before we accepted His gift of salvation. He loved us even when we were totally alienated from Him. And nothing we do now can ever separate us from His love. (Look again at Romans 8:38-39.) He will love us completely for all of eternity!

WHEN WE TURN AWAY FROM OUR SIN, GOD OFFERS US CLEANSING

But there's another aspect of forgiveness of which we don't often take advantage. Let me try to illustrate it for you.

One day Matthew came bolting into the house clutching something in his grubby little hands.

"Hey, hold up! What's that in your hands?" I wanted to know before whatever it was got all over the living room couch.

"Jellybeans," he replied, extending two very sticky, multi-colored appendages.

"Well, go wash your hands right now before we end up with psychedelic walls," I commanded.

After giving me a sideways, I-don't-know-why-Moms-are-so-picky look, he disappeared into the bathroom. I heard the water splashing and a sound I presumed was the bar of soap plopping onto the tile floor. A few minutes later he headed out the back door again.

"Hey, wait a minute, what's that you're holding now?" I hollered after him.

"My jellybeans," he hollered back.

"I thought I asked you to wash your hands," I responded, puzzled.

"I did!" he replied, staring at me blankly.

I stared back.

"You never said I had to get rid of the jellybeans!" he garbled as he stuffed them into his mouth, wiped his hands on his shirt, and picked up his Frisbee.

By then he was too far away for me to carry on any more of our conversation, so I just walked into the bathroom, picked up the colorful bar of soap, and mopped up the water that was all over the floor — in preparation for the next dirty kid.

You know, so often when we sin we do exactly what Matthew did with the jellybeans. We ask God to forgive us, and as soon as He does, we turn around and pick that sin right back up. Our cleaned-up lives immediately get sticky and grubby all over again.

God doesn't want to merely forgive our sins and temporarily clean up the mess they've left behind. He wants to get rid of them completely and purify our lives once and for all. First John 1:9 doesn't stop with forgiveness. I only read you the first half of the verse before. Let's read the whole thing: "If we confess our sins, he is faithful and just and will forgive us our sins *and purify us from all unrighteousness*" (emphasis added). God wants to clean and disinfect our lives.

We just read what David said about forgiveness in Psalm 103:3. But let's look at what he said in the context of the next two verses: "(God) forgives all (my) sins and heals all (my) diseases. *(He) redeems (my) life from the pit and crowns (me) with love and compassion, who satisfies (my) desires with good things so that (my) youth is renewed like the eagle's*" (emphasis added).

God doesn't want to stop at forgiveness. Look back at David's words. He doesn't want to just lift us up out of the pits of life into which we've sunk. He wants to crown our lives with love and compassion. He wants to set us apart as His sons and daughters. Our Father wants people to recognize that we are children of the King of the Universe when they see His love and compassion displayed in our lives. He also wants to satisfy our desires with *good* things, not the bad things that leave us hurting and hungry. And He doesn't want us to miss out on any of the enjoyment He planned for us, especially in our youth! He wants to restore us to a place where we can look back with joy at all of our years.

WHEN WE ARE FORGIVEN AND CLEANSED BY GOD, OUR LIVES BECOME BRAND NEW

God forgives us when we repent and ask Him for His forgiveness. But we also must be willing to forgive ourselves. The Bible contains countless illustrations of people whose lives were filled with huge sins, yet because of God's forgiveness and cleansing, they were made whole and clean. I immediately think of Rahab the harlot, who put her trust in the God of Israel (see Joshua 2) and became an ancestor in the genealogy of Jesus Christ (see Matthew 1:5). And how about Saul, who became famous for torturing and murdering Christians? When he met Christ on the road to Damascus, his life was completely transformed (see Acts 9:1-6), and he became God's spokesman to the Gentile nation. God later changed his name to Paul.

We must not look at our past with emotions of guilt or anger. We must not gaze at the present with feelings of despair. What appears to us beyond hope of repair, isn't! God is powerful enough to redeem any situation. Romans 8:28 tells us that He causes *all* things to work together for good to those who love Him. That includes *all the good* and *all the bad* things that can ever happen to us or that we can ever do.

In Isaiah 43:18-19 God tells us, "Forget the former things; do not dwell on the past. See, I am doing a new thing!" Our obligation is to give God everything — all our hurts, all our hungers, all our humiliations — and let Him transform our lives. He did it for Rahab the harlot and Saul the murderer. He can do it for us, too.

If you find that you have difficulty accepting God's cleansing, you may need to get some help from a Christian counselor. Talk to someone who understands the forgiveness that God offers for sin and who can guide you to a place of freshness and freedom. Seek out someone who can help you take your eyes off yourself and teach you to look straight into God's eyes, so that you can see for yourself His love and forgiveness.

God has wonderful plans for your life, no matter where it has already been. "'For I know the plans I have for you,' declares the Lord, 'plans to prosper you and not to harm you, plans to give you hope and a future'" (Jeremiah 29:11).

SUMMARY

We can do nothing to ever make God love us any more or any less than He already does. But the choices we make can drastically affect how much we enjoy His love. When we ignore God's standards, we reap consequences. Sin can distance us from God. It can distort our concept of Him. It can destroy our confidence and damage our conscience.

But God offers us forgiveness. If we agree with Him that it was wrong to violate His standards, He promises that He will forgive us. But He wants to do so much more than that. God wants to cleanse us and allow us to start all over with lives that are fresh and clean.

God wants to forgive us, and we must be willing to forgive ourselves as well. We don't have to live with guilt and pain or despair. We may need to seek godly counsel to help us really grasp the wonderful plans God has for our lives.

DISCUSSION QUESTIONS

DILEMMA #1: AREN'T RIGHT AND WRONG REALLY UP TO THE
INDIVIDUAL?

1. Explain how some of the measurements or standards we
   have established in our society point to the existence of a
   "Higher Source of Standards." (Use, for example, standards
   for time, distance, or space.)
2. What is the difference between a subjective, personal,
   moral standard and an objective, universal, moral
   standard?
3. Why do you think our culture has chosen to believe that
   there are no objective, universal standards when it comes
   to moral behavior?
4. If we truly believed that the determination of "Right and
   Wrong" was up to the individual, what would our society
   look like?
5. What are two "proofs" that God exists? Explain them.
6. How has God chosen to reveal His standards to us?

DILEMMA #2: WHY SHOULD I LIVE A MORAL LIFE IN SUCH AN
IMMORAL SOCIETY?

1. What was the only restriction God gave Adam and Eve in
   the Garden of Eden? Why did He make this restriction?
2. Why did God later have to add more restrictions (standards
   for living) in the lives of His people?

3. In what ways do God's standards set us free?

4. What three characteristics of God should make us willing to accept any standards that He designs?

5. What are some things that keep us from wanting to obey God's standards?

6. Read Psalm 1. According to this psalm, how does obeying God's standards affect our lives?

DILEMMA #3: *HOW* CAN I LIVE A MORAL LIFE IN SUCH AN IMMORAL SOCIETY?

1. Why does God allow the weeds to stay in His wheat field until harvest time?

2. Other than Rahab or Saul, can you think of a person in the Bible who looked like a weed at one time, but turned out to be a wonderful stalk of wheat? Can you think of a person who chose to remain a weed all his or her life?

3. How is the Holy Spirit like the motor in a vacuum cleaner?

4. What is the purpose of prayer in our lives?

5. If you were Satan, how would you keep people from plugging into the power available through prayer?

6. Why do we need other Christians in our lives? (Reread Hebrews 10:24-25.)

7. Read James 1:2-4. What do you think is the difference between happiness and joy?

DILEMMA #4: EXACTLY HOW HONEST AM I SUPPOSED TO BE?

1. Why did Halima choose to lie? What should she have done instead?

2. In what ways does complete honesty protect us?

3. What do you think the difference is between dishonesty and deceit? How does God view each of them?

4. How does understanding who God is help us with any honesty dilemma we might face?

5. In what area of your life do you struggle most with being honest?

DILEMMA #5: WHAT ABOUT SEX — HOW FAR IS TOO FAR?

1. God is totally pure and He exhibits only true love. How should these characteristics be displayed in our dating relationships?

2. What is the difference between lust and love? Why can all premarital sex be described as lust instead of love?

3. How does remaining sexually pure in our relationships protect us?

4. How has our culture made it difficult to stay within God's boundaries when it comes to sex?

5. What are some things that you can and should do to keep yourself sexually pure?

6. Write down a list of decisions that will keep you pure in your dating relationships. Are you willing to sign it?

DILEMMA #6: ISN'T HOMOSEXUALITY A VALID LIFESTYLE
ALTERNATIVE?

1. What is the difference between homosexual feelings and homosexual behavior?

2. What kinds of life experiences can lead a person to feelings of homosexuality?

3. What are some steps that a person who experiences homosexual feelings should take to avoid violating God's standards?

4. How would you respond to a person who argues that homosexuality is
   a. a "natural" instinct?
   b. a genetic condition?
   c. a harmless option?

5. How should Christians respond to people who practice homosexuality?

DILEMMA #7: WHAT'S THE BIG DEAL ABOUT ABORTION?
ISN'T IT A WOMAN'S RIGHT TO DECIDE WHAT
TO DO WITH HER OWN BODY?

1. Explain this statement: "A child who enters this world has been invited. He or she is not an intruder."

2. Read Psalm 139:13-16. What do you learn about God's view of life in the womb from these verses?

3. Why do you think our society seems to get more upset over the destruction of a swan's eggs than a child in the womb?

4. When does a woman have the right to choose whether or not to have a child?

5. What can Christians do to help save the lives of babies who will otherwise be aborted?

DILEMMA #8: CAN'T I JUST SEE FOR MYSELF WHAT'S WRONG
WITH DRUGS AND ALCOHOL? I WON'T BECOME
ADDICTED!

1. Why does God forbid us to do anything harmful to our bodies?

2. Because God created things like marijuana and the hops we use to make beer, how can it be wrong to use them?

3. Why do so many teenagers become involved with drinking and drugs?

4. How do all excesses and addictions become family affairs?

5. What are some of the lies that teenagers are led to believe about drinking and drugs?

6. How can you avoid becoming involved in the teenage culture of drinking and drugs?

DILEMMA #9: WHY ARE YOU SO CONCERNED ABOUT OUR MUSIC, MODEMS, AND THE MEDIA? IT'S ONLY ENTERTAINMENT!

1. How should the Holy Spirit's presence in our lives make a difference?

2. How clean is the Holy Spirit's workplace in your life?

3. What area of your mind do you think the Holy Spirit wants you to clean up the most?

4. How can you make yourself more aware of the presence of the Holy Spirit in your life?

5. Start a one-day journal of the music, modem, and media activity in your life, as described on page 140. Based on Matthew 22:37 and the results of your one-day journal, with how much of your mind do you love the Lord your God?

DILEMMA #10: WHAT IF I'VE ALREADY BLOWN IT?

1. Why does God allow us to experience painful consequences when we make wrong choices?

2. How do our choices affect our *relationship* with God?

3. How do our choices affect our *fellowship* with God?

4. What is the difference between forgiveness and cleansing?

5. When is it sometimes helpful to seek the guidance of a Christian counselor or psychologist?

6. Read Zephaniah 3:17. What does this verse mean to you personally?

NOTES

DILEMMA #1: AREN'T RIGHT AND WRONG REALLY UP TO THE INDIVIDUAL?

1. C. S. Lewis, *Mere Christianity* (New York: Collier, 1952), pp. 19-20.
2. Josh McDowell and Bob Hostetler, *Right from Wrong* (Dallas: Word, 1994), p. 81.
3. Gwendolyn M. Diaz, *Sticking Up for What I Believe* (Colorado Springs, Colo.: NavPress, 2002), p. 17-27.

DILEMMA #2: *WHY* SHOULD I LIVE A MORAL LIFE IN SUCH AN IMMORAL SOCIETY?

1. Vernard Eller, *The Mad Morality* (Nashville: Abingdon, 1970), p. 8.

DILEMMA #4: EXACTLY HOW HONEST AM I SUPPOSED TO BE?

1. Josh McDowell and Bob Hostetler, *Right from Wrong* (Dallas: Word, 1994), p. 175.
2. McDowell and Hostetler, p. 179.

DILEMMA #5: WHAT ABOUT SEX — HOW FAR IS TOO FAR?

1. Quoted by Charles Colson, *Answers to Your Kids' Questions* (Wheaton, Ill.: Tyndale, 2000), p. 130.
2. Quoted by Josh McDowell, *Love, Dad* (Dallas: Word, 1988), p. 53.

3. Peter Kreeft, *Making Choices* (Ann Arbor, Mich.: Servant Books, 1990), p. 97.

4. McDowell, p. 106.

DILEMMA #6: ISN'T HOMOSEXUALITY A VALID LIFESTYLE ALTERNATIVE?

1. Stephen Arterburn and Jim Burns, *Parents Guide to Top 10 Dangers Teens Face* (Wheaton, Ill.: Tyndale, 1995), pp. 191-193.

2. Charles Colson, *Answers to Your Kids' Questions* (Wheaton, Ill.: Tyndale, 2000), p. 117.

3. Dr. James Dobson, *Life on the Edge* (Dallas: Word, 1995), p. 223.

DILEMMA #7: WHAT'S THE BIG DEAL ABOUT ABORTION? ISN'T IT A WOMAN'S RIGHT TO DECIDE WHAT TO DO WITH HER OWN BODY?

1. Charles Colson, *Answers to Your Kids' Questions* (Wheaton, Ill.: Tyndale, 2000), p. 144.

2. Colson, pp. 140-141.

3. Reardon Elliott Institute, online source.

4. Reardon Elliot Institute, online source.

ABOUT THE
AUTHOR

GWENDOLYN MITCHELL DIAZ began life as a missionary kid in Nigeria, but moved to the United States at age ten. A graduate of the University of Pennsylvania, she spent many years working in the medical profession and writing articles and columns about sports, family, and her faith in God. She also has published the books *The Adventures of Mighty Mom, Mighty Mom's Secrets for Raising Super Kids,* and *Sticking Up for What I Believe* (NavPress).

As a mother of four boys, Gwen feels particularly passionate about helping teens solidify their faith and grow as Christians. *Sticking Up for What Is Right* practically defines the standards God has established for their lives. It points out the wisdom of abiding by these standards and provides solutions for the difficulties they will encounter when they don't. Gwen is able to communicate Christianity to teens in a way that will capture their interest, satisfy their curiosity, and convey God's exciting truths.